Haier purpose

Haier
purpose

The real story of China's first global super-company

Hu Yong & Hao Yazhou

**with an introduction by
Des Dearlove & Stuart Crainer**

A Thinkers50 publication
in association with Infinite Ideas

Copyright © Haier, 2017

The right of Haier to be identified as the authors of this book has been asserted in accordance with the Copyright, Designs and Patents Act 1988.

First published in English in 2017 by
Infinite Ideas Limited
36 St Giles
Oxford
OX1 3LD
United Kingdom
www.infideas.com

Originally published as Haier's innovation journey: 1984–2014

A CIP catalogue record for this book is available from the British Library
ISBN 978–1–908984–85–2
Brand and product names are trademarks or registered trademarks of their respective owners.

Printed in Britain

Contents

Preface: A letter to makers

by Zhang Ruimin, Chairman and CEO, Haier Group

Technical development is the key factor in increasing the prosperity of the human race. The development of our minds has driven all major leaps in civilization. Now the Internet has brought huge improvements to our technical resources and we stand at a critical juncture. Large-scale industry will develop so that each individual will become a part of a machine, moving along new paths of development; zero distance, decentralization, and distributed Internet thinking are taking us into an era full of new prospects and challenges.

After 30 years of innovation and development, Haier has grown from a small, almost bankrupt, collectively owned factory to today's leading brand in global white goods. Globally, Haier has hundreds of millions of users, and every day, hundreds of thousands of Haier products are put onto the market. The advances in human industry have created today's Haier, allowing us to undergo the 100 years of development experienced by traditional enterprises in advanced economies in just 30 years. We hope to be regarded as a classic example of business development, and also stand as a benchmark for others to learn from. Faced with new challenges, our only weapon is that we have never abandoned the founding spirit of innovation – Haier is always entrepreneurial, always innovative.

An emperor once asked his ministers the difference between entrepreneurship and conservatism, in other words, originating as opposed to maintaining. The ministers' answer was that while starting a business is hard, maintaining it is even harder. The answer of Haier's corporate culture to this question is that entrepreneurship and maintenance should not be thought of as separate things, the only way forward is to maintain entrepreneurship.

The spirit of entrepreneurship is the successful experience and mindset described in the classic Chinese text, *Dao De Jing* – to defeat the enemy requires strength, but defeating the self makes you the true winner. The essence of the culture of Haier is that we do not rest on our laurels.

This is true not only of the company but for every individual involved in Haier. In the Internet era, everyone is their own CEO, everyone should become an entrepreneur.

The Chinese word for 'entrepreneur' is just slightly different to the Chinese word for a business, yet there is a world of difference in meaning and essence. Businesses are business-centric, whereas entrepreneurs are user-centric. The mission of enterprises is to create perfect products and services, whereas the mission of entrepreneurs is to create the best possible experience for users. Enterprises use size and profits as their tools, whereas entrepreneurs use user resources and loyal fans as theirs. Enterprises use management and control, whereas entrepreneurs use their own unique set of tools. Each individual innovation can lead to the creation of a new company.

In Haier's early days, our contribution to the community was branded products. Later we provided Haier branded services to the community. Haier then elected to transition from a closed hierarchical organization to an open business platform, from a walled garden to an ecosystem containing many new makers and enterprises. Today, we offer our resources to society, providing a Haier branded business platform to makers. This means that those innovators who are full of entrepreneurial passion, can develop new products within the Haier platform.

We have also opened our supply chain resources to the public, so each supplier and user can participate in Haier's new processes and create user value. In doing this, Haier has created the new soil in which innovation can grow, and the results will be equal opportunities and fairness for everyone, with all stakeholders building a win–win situation.

Since 2005, Haier has been applying the 'individual goals together' business model. We have given up the simple pursuit of traditional business results. In the absence of benchmarks, we endure questioning and criticism from the outside world, but we are determined to persevere, not just with the aim of success, but in the spirit of exploration.

To mark the tenth anniversary of the Haier venture, in 1994, I wrote an article called 'Haier is the Sea'. Now, I envisage Haier as a cloud, as, no matter how large the sea, it still has edges. But even the smallest cloud can drift anywhere.

Open, open, and reopen. More than 100 small companies have been bred and hatched on Haier's cloud platform. They have left Haier to form stand-alone entrepreneurial enterprises. There are also social entrepreneurs making use of the Haier Internet platform to create businesses. They deserve respect, and I would like to thank them. Because Haier's entrepreneurial platform transition itself is an innovation; the Haier platform does not have the 30-year history of Haier, but is a newborn baby, a rising sun. The makers on the Haier platform are both the entrepreneurs and the builders of our platform.

I would like to pay tribute to the great era of makers! Haier strives to be a home and a community for great makers.

Introduction

Stuart Crainer & Des Dearlove

The organizations which are managed in the most effective and innovative ways are likely to outperform their competitors. Management can be a competitive advantage.

This is the basis of the concept of 'management innovation', championed by London Business School's Gary Hamel and Julian Birkinshaw. From Toyota's lean manufacturing to the Malaysian government's embrace of blue ocean strategy, organizations of all types are constantly seeking out new and better ways to manage their resources. The job of managers is to improve the performance of the resources they have and to identify the future resources they need.

Increasingly, the vital importance of management is being appreciated by the largest organizations of our times. The challenges now faced by companies such as Facebook, Apple and Google are fundamentally about management. They have all developed groundbreaking technology, now the challenge is to maximize the social and economic impact of that technology. This is a management challenge.

Management has unfortunately received a bad press. Managers are synonymous in some sectors with bureaucrats. In large public sector organizations especially managers are often regarded with suspicion. They are the bean-counters, faceless men and women with their spreadsheets. In fast growing high-tech companies the managers are the guys in the suits brought in to be the grown-ups while the smart guys in jeans and t-shirts get into the sexy world of bright ideas and even brighter cutting edge products.

But without management, organizations grind unceremoniously to a halt. It takes management for organizations to grow and develop.

Who are the managers?

If we accept that management is important then who are the managers? Who actually practises management?

Over the last century or more the emphasis has been on professionalizing management, to bring the discipline, status and rewards of the professional to the art and science of management. This has had benefits. Managers are better educated than previously. They fill lecture theatres at business schools, have created the booming executive education market and absorb the constant influx of new ideas from business books, magazines and online talks. Managers know their stuff.

The trouble with this, however, is that management has become exclusive rather than the naturally inclusive activity it needs to be to really succeed. Professional managers, with their MBAs and their bookshelves creaking with insights, have a vested interest in keeping their professional domain safe from interlopers. Turkeys tend not to vote for Christmas.

The reality is that someone with a brilliant idea on the factory floor as to how the organization could better use its resources is unlikely to be heard. This is as true now, with a few glorious exceptions, as it was 100 years ago. In too many organizations, management stops people managing.

This, we believe, is slowly changing and will need to continue to change. Management will go through a necessary recalibration in order to maximize the new resources at the disposal of managers and organizations. This requires five key realizations:

1. **Management is organic.** The best management is not the

result of intricate processes, labyrinthine spreadsheets, and minute measurements. These things are important, but management is as much an art as a science. There is no universal formula. People are at the heart of management and people must be given the freedom to manage themselves and for the nature of their own management style to evolve.

2. **Management is open.** One of the big ideas of the last decade has been Open Innovation. The classic example of this is Procter & Gamble which threw its innovation doors open to embrace ideas from customers, suppliers, and others outside the organization. This is laudable and productive. No one company has a monopoly on wisdom. Apply the same idea to management. No organization has a monopoly on managerial wisdom. Nor does one department, sector or team. The more open to management ideas an organization is the more likely it is to discover the power of management as a competitive advantage.

3. **Management is free of hierarchy.** In the 1990s Tom Peters sounded a colourful death knell for middle managers. He proclaimed they were 'cooked geese'. If only. Recently we were working with a company in Silicon Valley in which there was a cadre of middle managers intent on inaction. Their colleagues labelled them 'zombies', but in this particular part of the Valley the zombies ruled. Look around now and you will discover that middle managers are alive and well inside our large organizations. Indeed, look inside many smaller organizations and you will encounter needless levels of management. All managers need to justify their existence in terms of the value they add to the organization's activities. Simply holding down a place in a hierarchy justifies nothing.

4. **Management maximizes technology.** It is interesting how many organizations we visit where the very latest technology is utilized on the factory floor or in the company's interactions with customers and users, but not in its management.

Technology sets managers free. It enables more flexible, more global, more interactive, more open, more challenging management than ever before. The best managers we have encountered embrace technology fulsomely.

5. **The units of management are small.** At its best, the units of management should be limited in size and unlimited in ambition. Small, flexible teams enabled by technology are the modus operandi of the most innovative companies – in their research and development labs at least – but often difficult to find elsewhere in the organizations. A company board is a small team. The C-suite is a locker room. And that stretches up and down an organization: teams are management Viagra.

Alongside this recalibration of management so that it actually delivers what organizations need and want is a questioning of the very nature of organizations.

The context in which management is practised is the organization.

Management and the organization exist in tandem. Neither should be static. Organizations constantly change shape and direction – or, at least, they should.

As with management, the organizations of the world largely remain structured as they were 100 years ago. In the Internet age industrial organizations embedded in the structures and expectations of the past remain dominant. Don't be taken in by the window dressing (in the form of free food, relaxed dress codes and so on); the modern corporation is rigidly structured. It may not have the elaborate organizational charts of yesterday, but it remains remorselessly linear in its structure and thinking.

The modern corporation worked in the twentieth century. Then the emphasis was on size, benefiting from the new vistas of scale made available by the assembly line and mass production. Growing bigger justified the existence of the twentieth-century corporation. This is no longer the case. A company's headcount can no longer be equated with its commercial health and likely longevity. Companies die and slow-moving giants are no exception. Size insulates an organization, but only from the changes necessary to keep it alive.

Research suggests that individuals who experience self-doubt are actually more successful. Apply the same logic to managers and organizations and we believe you will begin to understand what is necessary to compete in the future. The best will question themselves and every aspect of what they do and why.

As you will see, Haier and its remarkable CEO Zhang Ruimin have been asking questions of how they manage and the nature of their organization for many years. 'There is no successful company, only those which stay relevant,' Zhang Ruimin told us when we met at Haier's headquarters in Qingdao, China. 'There is no end to exploration of business models and management thinking. You have to challenge yourself. Can you remain relevant in changing times?'

Zhang Ruimin is a humble man. This is expressed in his modest bearing and in his relentless curiosity. He is the best read business leader we have ever encountered. He knows his Mintzberg from his Hamel, his Handy from his Kanter. He wants to improve himself and his organization.

This appears trivial and you would think it is commonplace. It isn't. Many senior managers we encounter appear hell-bent on securing their legacy or stock options rather than improving their own performance and that of their organization. They are as likely to discuss the latest ideas on innovation as they are to abseil down the headquarters building. There are, of course, exceptions, but humility and curiosity do tend to be in short-supply in the Western corporate world.

Haier's story is unique, but its lessons are universal and hugely challenging. The company has come from truly ramshackle origins to take over GE Appliances, part of corporate America's greatest modern empire. It has changed the way management is practised and it should change the way managers throughout the world think about their jobs.

So far Haier has managed to pass the relevance test posed by its own CEO. Its story is a remarkable one, and one we acknowledged by giving the Thinkers50 Ideas into Practice Award to Haier and Zhang Ruimin. But it is not the story of one man nor a single company, it is the story of how management and organizations can and must change if they are to shape the future.

Stuart Crainer and Des Dearlove
March 2017

Before Haier
(1978–1983)

Chinese pragmatism

China's economic reform was first pioneered in the countryside. One night in November 1978, in a small village in Xiaohe Township, Fengyang County, Chuzhou, Anhui Province, 18 villagers braved the risk of jail, and marked their red handprints on contract documents. China's countryside had started on its historic transformation from the people's commune system to the household contract responsibility system. From the beginning, this reform was driven by the margins.

In their book *How China Became Capitalist*, Ronald Coase and Ning Wang present a systematic review of China's reform. They believe that there were actually two Chinese reforms: one being the reform promoted by the Chinese government, the other being the revolution in the margins. The real change in China's economics, the pressure that led to the reintroduction of market forces and entrepreneurial spirit was this marginal revolution. The reform introduced collective, household and township enterprises, and also included self-employment and the creation of the Shenzhen Special Economic Zone. Although these forces existed only on the margins of socialism, they were the main factors in

China's economic reform.

Practicality is the core philosophy of China's reform and opening up. The reform emerged out of problems, but it is also deepened in the continuous solution to problems.

Economic transformation

In September 1978, Deng Xiaoping conducted his inspection tour of the northeast. He visited a lot of enterprises, and began to consider the more far-reaching problems of China's businesses. He said: 'What I want to emphasize is that we should quickly and resolutely shift our focus to economic construction.'

In December 1978, at the Third Plenary Session of the Eleventh Communist Party Congress, the focus of the country was shifted to the strategic policy of socialist modernization, breaking the dominance of the mandatory plan approach, and allowing the gradual introduction of market mechanisms and the recognition of market competition. China had started its transition from being a planned economy to becoming a modern market economy. Economist Zhang Wuchang called this transformation 'the greatest economic reform programme'. A new social class – Chinese entrepreneurs – began to form and rise against this backdrop. This movement towards the new economy happened gradually, and the commercial landscape formed slowly.

Opening up

All social change needs a leading edge. Deng Xiaoping stated that 'before making a unified national programme, we can start from local regions, starting the new system from one region or industry, gradually opening up. Central departments allow and encourage local regions to carry out such trials.' In April 1979, Deng Xiaoping put forward the idea of pilot Special Zones: 'We can set aside a place, called a Special Zone, to blaze a new trail.' Under Deng Xiaoping's initiative, the CPC Central Committee and the State Council decided to create pilot Special Zones in Shenzhen,

Zhuhai, Shantou in Guangdong and Xiamen in Fujian. In May 1980, according to Deng Xiaoping's proposal, the existing Export Zones were renamed Special Economic Zones. On 25 August 1980, the NPC Standing Committee passed the Guangdong Province Special Economic Zone Ordinance, marking the official birth of Special Economic Zones in China.

Household electronics

From 1978 onwards, the previously closed doors of Chinese business opened to the world and some of the world's top managers and business leaders visited China.

Kōnosuke Matsushita's first visit was made in 1979. His ambition was to aid the development of the Chinese electronics industry by working with the manufacturers of Japan. In the same month, Akio Morita, head of Sony, also visited China.

On 27 December 1979, Panasonic products appeared in the windows of a Beijing Department Store, marketed with the slogan, 'We can improve cultural life by adopting home appliances'. A beautiful young model stood in the window display. She held a tea tray in her hands and was surrounded by television sets, refrigerators, washing machines, stereos and the other appliances of the modern home environment. This showed people a picture of a new, wonderful family life. Above the window the Chinese name of Panasonic was written in bright characters.

This window was a real window to the outside world for the Chinese people who had just left their closed society. Although it was criticized immediately as 'promoting high consumption and a capitalist way of life', with one critic even posting a note on the glass stating 'this is downright traitorous', this did not stop the enthusiasm for these appliances. Japanese TVs became extremely popular and Japanese electronics helped the Chinese people learn about the world.

One Sanyo-branded tape recorder was what many young women dreamed of getting as their dowry, along with the sunglasses and bell-bottoms, which constituted the sartorial standard for fashionable youth. Many years later, the Sanyo home appliances business was acquired by a Chinese company – Haier.

Japanese-style management

Alongside the arrival of modern appliances, the equally important Japanese-style of management also entered China. The 'God of Management', Kōnosuke Matsushita was the first Japanese businessperson to draw public attention in China. As the founder of Panasonic, he pioneered divisions, career-long employment, the seniority-wage system and other Japanese enterprise management systems.

From 1949 to just before the economic reform, China did not have modern management based around free enterprise or market performance. At that stage, China had a highly centralized planned economy, based on public ownership. The role of businesses was to serve as workshops undertaking production tasks. The management of the enterprise was entirely based around the management of production.

An interesting element in this is the differing interpretations of Frederick Taylor's scientific management system, which he developed early in the twentieth century. It was severely criticized in Russia and China as the capitalist way of brutalizing the working class. In April 1918, Lenin, in his article 'Immediate Tasks of the Soviet Government', noted that capitalism had created employment and organizational systems which essentially enslaved working people, yet, at the same time raised the productivity of labour. He singled out Taylorism as a system which the workers hated but which represented tremendous progress in terms of analysing the process of production and hugely increasing productivity. Lenin wanted to introduce the Taylor system within the Socialist Soviet Republic in a way that was not harmful to the workers.

In the 1980s, when China started its economic reform, Lenin's idea of adapting Taylorism was used to promote not only the introduction of Western production lines, but also the introduction of Western management. But Taylor's core theories tended to create rigid corporate cultures. In contrast, Matsushita's 'flexible management' was more in line with the ideas of Chinese entrepreneurs. He became the first international icon for Chinese entrepreneurs. After him, Kyocera's Kazuo Inamori, Sony's Akio Morita, Toyota's Taiichi Ohno and Soichiro Honda became role models for Chinese business managers.

Matsushita and other Japanese entrepreneurs allowed Chinese entrepreneurs to understand the role of companies in national economic revitalization, inspiring that generation of Chinese entrepreneurs to believe that 'industry can serve the country'.

American-style management

When Matsushita and Akio Morita visited China in 1979, most Chinese did not know even the very basics of management, and did not understand the international market at all. At that time Japan was on the rise. Capitalizing on the 1970s oil crisis, Japanese cars, with their low fuel consumption, had broken into the US market. At the same time, in high-tech fields, Japanese electronics companies gradually overtook their American competitors. The Toyota Production System became the production model of choice. Just in time, automation, Kanban methods, standardized work, lean production management and other concepts became popular in the business community.

Also in 1979, Harvard professor Ezra Vogel published *Japan as Number One: Lessons for America*. Two years later, another American expert William Ouchi used Japanese companies as a blueprint in his book *Theory Z: How American Business Can Meet the Japanese Challenge*, which was among the first books to emphasize the importance of corporate culture. Ouchi said that the essence of corporate management in Japan is people-oriented, and the rights of production for each employee are respected. He warned American enterprises: 'Our enemy is not the Japanese, but the limitations of corporate management culture.'

In that year, suffering from the impact of Japanese competition, the US automobile maker Chrysler encountered a serious management crisis. Lee Iacocca became president, turning the tide, and becoming a hero of US industry. Two years later, in 1981, 42-year-old Jack Welch became GE's CEO. His American management system swept the business world.

Japan absorbed quality management thoughts from America, but attached great importance to allowing enterprises to go the Japanese way. Japanese companies were formed on the basis of traditional Japanese culture, absorbing the advanced experience of the West to create a unique management style. Generally, US corporate management remains more focused on technology, equipment, systems, methods, organizational structure and other hard factors, whereas Japanese companies place more emphasis on people, goals, beliefs, values and other soft factors. Japanese employees have the concept of loving their workplace in the same way as they love their own homes. American corporate employees do not share this concept.

The Japanese–American cultural battle over management styles quickly came to the fore of the Chinese world of commerce. At the time the Japanese 'Gods of Business' were at their peak, US-based companies such as Coca-Cola began to covet the Chinese market. In 1979, 30,000 boxes of Coca-Cola were shipped from Hong Kong to Beijing, Shanghai and Guangzhou and other large shopping malls and hotels. Coca-Cola's Chinese campaign had officially started. Coca-Cola brought many features which were eye-opening for Chinese enterprises: they carried out modern China's first store promotion activity, placed advertising to establish their brand image, and subsequently implemented localization operations.

From this perspective, China's first batch of pioneering entrepreneurs were lucky, as they were able to receive the wisdom of both Japanese and US management cultures at the same time.

The birth of enterprises

In March 1978, Deng Xiaoping said that:

A problem slowing our progress is that there is no awareness of how to manage. Backward technology, low levels of technology management, and other factors are very prominent problems for industry. If we say that socialism is superior to capitalism, then we should manage better than capitalists. Improving the scientific and technological level and management level is very important. There is a huge difference between good and bad management. We are faced with an extremely important problem, which is the management problem. In fact, we Chinese do not know how to manage.

At the beginning of the 1980s, after his visit to China, Japanese economist Ryutaro Komiya made the surprise announcement that in his view China had no enterprises. By 1987, Deng Xiaoping could say: 'We did not expect the largest harvest; it was caused by the development of township enterprises.'

Township enterprises were a means of putting collective productions onto the market. They started to develop from 1979 onwards, and then they experienced two peaks from 1984 to 1988 and 1992 to 1998, becoming the most active portion of China's economy. Wing Thye Woo, Hai Wen and Jin Yibiao pointed out in their article 'How Successful has Chinese Enterprise Reform Been?': 'The biggest achievement was the birth and rapid growth of China's township enterprises.'

Various models of development of township enterprises emerged, such as the Sunan model, Wenzhou model, Jinjiang model, and Pearl River Delta model. In the new century, these development models underwent fundamental changes, and some were fully replaced by new private enterprises. China's private economy appeared from scratch, from few to many, from small to large, starting in the self-employed economy, growing into a private sector. From the original state-owned, collective enterprise, mixed economy engine, the country gradually transitioned to having three engines of commerce: state-owned, private and foreign investment, and the share of the private economy was expanding.

This commercial development spawned a variety of organizational forms. Institutions and state-owned enterprises still existed, but alongside private enterprises, multinational companies and various other social organizations. On this basis of organizational pluralism, Chinese people were reorganized, and began the transition from the familiar but closed work units (*danwei*), courtyards and villages towards openness and diversification.

Zhang Ruimin – The beginning

Zhang Ruimin was born in Qingdao in January 1949. During the Cultural Revolution he was a 'laosanjie' – a student who graduated during the particularly turbulent late 1960s. He followed in his father's footsteps, as a manual worker. He then served as team leader, workshop director, director, and Qingdao Home Appliances company vice-manager under the Second Bureau of Light Industry Appliance. In December 1984, he joined Qingdao Daily Appliance Plant – the predecessor of today's Haier Group, where he served as workshop director.

The main reasons why I had to come to Haier were that I was working class but that I had been through school education, 'red' education, patriotic education. The focus of the education was that we must do something for the country, and must not be mediocre.

Of course, I never had an opportunity to do that. As a working class young man, what chances did I ever have? Let's take the Cultural Revolution period as an example; the opportunities were either college or military service. Both required that somebody 'open a back door' for you (i.e. you needed personal connections). In fact, at that time, even in a work unit you had to go through the back door to enjoy certain opportunities. But for me these were all impossible.

So when the Cultural Revolution led to the closure of the

college, until I joined the factory, I had never thought I would be able to do anything at all. I really did not want to waste time, but I had no chances, so I studied mechanical manufacturing and the like by myself. In the factory I made some little technological innovations. What I had was time, I was able to borrow books and read a lot. At that time, I was reading a lot of biographies, for example, Napoleon, but I had no opportunities.

Then all of a sudden I joined the appliance company, not physically inside the factory, and I really wanted to do something meaningful, but there really was nothing I could do. I just went to work, read the newspaper, had meetings and so on. I took a team to West Germany to introduce their technology and equipment to China, I did not think of coming to a refrigerator plant. But for this introduction project, I had to go to Beijing, run the project, and arrange foreign exchange. The plant was not in good condition at that time. No one was managing these things. I was the leader of a division of the appliances company. Slowly, I started to develop feelings about the place. The factory had changed leadership three times in three years. The previous leader did not want to do it any more; he said that if we could not recruit more people, he would simply leave. Then he walked away. No one came. That was in 1984, and in May 1985 the equipment was ready to enter the plant. But after the German equipment was introduced, it was thrown into the yard and forgotten.

Anyway, although that step was not really my responsibility, partly because I had some feelings about the place, and again because of my childhood education, I was ready to fight for the socialist cause. In my childhood, we shouted together that we were ready. It sounds like an empty slogan, but that is what we did every day. In fact, I really felt I wanted to do something for the country and our nation. I cannot say I was thinking about all those things at the time, but I did have some ideas.

When this equipment was thrown into the yard, even if it was not my responsibility, the waste was also a loss to the nation. In fact, at that time, newspapers often reported that in many places imported equipment had been thrown away, as finally it turned into a pile of scrap metal. This kind of thing happened a lot, as no one was held responsible. So I looked into a number of potential candidates, who would come and who would not, but we really could not find anyone to come to the plant. Finally I said I would do it.

In fact, there was still a certain amount of risk in coming to the plant. My wages would be moved over from a stable job, so if I did not succeed, it would be like moving from a feast to a famine. At that time I was really scared, as I had concerns about my family. After setting things up, I called my wife on the telephone, I said I might go there, and that if I did not do well, I might well have to stay there, and that I would not be able to return. I said I would not care, I had been a manual worker in the past, so if I had to be one again, that would be fine, I could do it. My wife was also open about it, saying that it did not matter, if I could not do well there our little income was still enough to feed two people.

The birth of Haier (1984–1991)

1984 – Old thinking, new ideas

Thanks to George Orwell, in Europe and America, the year 1984 is synonymous with a totalitarian 'Big Brother'. But in China, 1984 saw a burst of vitality.

The Chinese economist Mao Yushi called 1984 the year when 'old thinking had no way out, but new ideas just sprang up.' The old thinking was still controlling the whole of society, only a handful of people had new ideas. For example, the non-state-owned economy, the private economy, were not mentioned then, but by the late 1980s, people began to talk about it.

At the beginning of the reform, the ambition of most Chinese workers was to have a stable job with government enterprises or institutions, which entitled them to enjoy a variety of benefits. This situation was commonly known as the iron rice bowl. However, with the deepening of the reform and opening up policy, after the mid-1980s, the phrase 'jumping into the sea' (meaning moving into the private sector) began to be heard.

Former news commentator for the *People's Daily* Ma Licheng commented on the transition: 'Citizens have more choices, as there is more space, so opportunities in social innovation and national innovation are appearing. This was the development of space, it was the development of freedom, it was the development of wealth, it was the development of capital, and it was the development of modernization.'

At the beginning of the 1980s, the self-employed Nian Guangjiu sold Shazi Sunflower Seeds in Wuhu, Anhui Province. In the beginning the company founder and his son employed four assistants; over two years, this developed into a private enterprise with an annual turnover of ¥7.2 million and 140 employees. This was contrary to the 1979 State Administration for Industry's 'No Private Employment' stipulation. At that time, the doctrine, derived from Marx's *Das Kapital*, was that hiring seven people or fewer in order to make money for your own consumption was considered to be self-employment; those with eight or more employees produced surplus value, and that was exploitation, with the operators being seen as capitalists.

Dispute raged from Wuhu to Beijing as Nian Guangjiu's story became the beginning of the discussion about capitalist restoration and exploitation. The City of Wuhu appointed staff to conduct an investigation and write a report to submit to the Central Committee. This alarmed Deng Xiaoping. On 22 October 1984, he stated: 'I would like to put this issue on the back burner for two years, and then look again, allowing Shazi Sunflower Seeds to do some business. What is there to be afraid of? Would it harm socialism?'

Then on 22 January 1987, the Communist Party of China decided 'to deepen rural reform', for the first time recognizing private enterprises. Private entrepreneurs were invited back to China. By 2013, China's private economy accounted for about 60 per cent of GDP.

The commodity economy

In October 1984, The Third Plenary Session of the Eleventh CPC adopted the Decision on Economic Reform, making it clear that China's socialist economy was to be a planned commodity economy based on public ownership. This was the first time the words 'commodity economy' were written into the Party's decisions, a change from the original 'planned economy supplemented by market regulation'. Today, the idea of the commodity economy can be seen as a transitional concept, but when the expression 'resources and products can be exchanged' was used for the first time, it was not easy.

'Some words have never been spoken by our ancestors; some were new words… in the past we could not have written such a document,' said Deng Xiaoping of the decision. The document broke with the idea that the planned economy and commodity economy were in conflict, and this laid the foundation for the later establishment of a market economy system. New values began to appear; 'competition' was no longer a derogatory term, nor was it seen as an inherently undesirable phenomenon of capitalism.

On 23 October 1985, when Deng Xiaoping met with a senior US business delegation organized by Time Inc., he said: 'Some areas and some people can get rich, leading and helping other areas and other people, so that we can gradually achieve common prosperity.' This was a break from the planned economy, which had gradually lost its vitality. China urgently needed some people to become rich, so as to demonstrate the effects of the market economy applied with Chinese characteristics.

Market economy theory gave a positive incentive to a number of capable entrepreneurs; they began to put their own soldiers on the battlefield based on the needs of their enterprises, and management, so they would be ready to jump into action.

The first year of the Chinese enterprise

At the beginning of the 1980s, China established a household contract responsibility system down to the level of villages and households. Contractual management rights were separated from those of farmers' collectives, following the terminology of the time, and the rights were split into two parts. MIT Sloan School professor Yasheng Huang said that in fact, this policy was a way of privatizing contract rights; 'the land contract policy was revolutionary, which was the most important start. Without that start, none of the following things would have been able to happen. There would be no Vanke, no Lenovo, and no people like Liu Chuanzhi. China's reforms mainly started from the rural areas, and then expanded into production, broadening the income base. This mechanism was then introduced into cities.' Although not very smooth, it played a very important role in breaking the rigidity of the urban system, and people like Liu Chuanzhi, the founder of Lenovo, declared that they were ready to move forward.

In 1984, the focus of China's reform moved from rural to urban areas. The main thrust of the first round of reforms was to expand on the autonomy of enterprises and the implementation of factory director responsibility. Zhejiang Haiyan Shirt Factory director Bu Xinsheng implemented a bonus system, becoming a model for the first wave of reformers; and Ma Shengli, contractor of the Shijiazhuang Paper Mill, started the journey to contracting for hundreds of state-owned enterprises.

This period also marked the first attempts at Chinese SOE reform. Rural collective enterprises were officially renamed township enterprises. Leaders moved towards economic development. Vanke in Shenzhen, Lenovo in Zhongguancun, Beijing, and Haier in Qingdao were all started. Thirty years later they had become the backbone of the Chinese business community, the unquestioned leaders in their respective industries.

Zhang Ruimin introduced the concept of quality to Chinese enterprise, by using a hammer to smash 76 sub-standard refrigerator units (more on this later). Company founder Li Jingwei, asked people to design the trademark for Jianlibao, and sponsored the first Chinese sports delegation on its return to the Olympics. This was the cutting edge of brand awareness for Chinese enterprises. When real estate developer Vanke started, it chased the various opportunities created by its diversification, but in the end, Wang Shi used residential specialization and scale to achieve the fast development of Vanke. When looking back at this time,

Lenovo founder Liu Chuanzhi said: 'Many other famous people also started along with me in 1984, including a lot of well-known entrepreneurs, but not many of them are still in their jobs today. In order to get things done, we had to consider the situation, and make big changes.' This generation of entrepreneurs shared the characteristic of having a restless and adventurous spirit. They quickly sensed the change in the political climate and seized the opportunities it presented.

Zhang Ruimin takes a sledgehammer to defective products, communicating the need for quality and respect for users

Booming foreign investments

In 1984, Deng Xiaoping visited Shenzhen and Zhuhai Special Economic Zones and affirmed the development of the Zones. This was the first of Deng Xiaoping's two famous visits to the south of China.

Two months later, the CPC Central Committee made a major decision, declaring that 'China would open fourteen coastal cities and Hainan Island to foreign investors'. China's openness to foreign investment spread, until eventually the entire coastal territory was open.

In that year, Shanghai Volkswagen Automotive Co. Ltd was set up, and DuPont, Kraft, 3M, Hill & Knowlton and other multinational companies also set up offices or companies in China. In 1986, the State Council issued Regulations on Encouraging Foreign Investment, and this became an important point in the history of opening China to foreign capital. It also happened to be in this year that China started GATT (the predecessor of the World Trade Organization) negotiations.

Before 1986, foreign investment was tentative. In 1986, after the State Council issued the Regulations, there was a substantial increase in the utilization of foreign investment for production projects and exports. Between 1986 and 1991, total foreign investment in China was $19 billion, three times more than the previous six years.

From that point, Santana cars assembled at the plant in Shanghai appeared on China's roads, Coca-Cola stopped being a rare product which could only be purchased with a foreign exchange certificate, KFC opened their doors in Beijing, becoming China's first fast-food restaurant, Nike shoes and blue jeans were widely welcomed. In terms of personal consumption, Chinese people gradually moved towards globalization.

The spending spree

Under the planned economy, there was a huge conflict between the circulation system and the nascent commodity economy. Consumer demand was growing daily, but at that time in China it was hard to buy anything and equally difficult to sell anything. There was a shortage of high-end household appliances; for some brand names, not only did you need to buy tickets you even needed to queue through the night. The enthusiasm of Chinese consumers was almost too much for some manufacturers. A Tokyo-based reporter calculated that so many orders were received by Guangzhou refrigerator plant in 1984 that at their then rate of production it would have taken at least 20 years to fulfil them.

Before opening its doors to the world, China's economy had not left the era of shortages. The vast majority of Chinese urban and rural families were still barely on the verge of having enough food and clothing, hundreds of millions of people were still struggling with poverty. There was a small group of more affluent people. There were also those who lived in frugal pursuit of the 'old three things' (bicycle, watch and sewing machine). After the mid-1980s, TVs, washing machines and refrigerators became the 'new three things'. These goods had popular channels to enter Chinese urban households.

Looking at refrigerators, for example, in 1984, the total output of Chinese refrigerators was 577,000 units, in 1985 this soared to 1.448 million units, and by 1988, this number had increased to a world-leading 7.576 million units.

Information economy

In 1984, as businesses in China prepared to face the complete overhaul of the country's economy, the global business revolution led by the information economy began to make waves. Harvard dropout Bill Gates wrote his own DOS system licensed to IBM and other PC makers. This software, named Microsoft, began a decades-long story of PC system domination.

Another school dropout Michael Dell assembled computer accessories in his dorm room as required by users, as a way to obtain business capital. Dell's direct sales model became a new entrepreneurial story.

At the same time, a couple of Stanford University teachers created the multi-protocol routing mode to connect each Stanford LAN. With routers as their main business, they began the development of networked devices; the enterprise they pioneered was called Cisco.

Peter Drucker

Over those seven years, the field of global business was also undergoing a quiet revolution. In 1985, Peter Drucker published *Innovation and Entrepreneurship*. The 'Master of Masters' put forward a new management paradigm, namely that innovation and entrepreneurship are fundamental business capabilities.

Throughout his life, Drucker tried to understand the increasing complexity of business and society, and how this complexity would affect the value of creation and distribution. From the 1960s and 1970s, great changes had been predicted: an information economy renaissance, work based around knowledge and various types of digital technology. These trends gradually became a reality in the 1980s; Drucker wrote numerous works emphasizing the changes in management practices. He knew that the transformations in the nature of work meant that the existing management practices and skills of workers would soon become obsolete, and that management must respond.

At that time Drucker was a name that the Chinese people did not know. However, a 30-year-old director accidentally got his hands on a book written by Drucker. He treasured it. From a dilapidated factory in the Shandong Peninsula, he pondered how an enterprise that was unable to pay its wages could get out of trouble. The director was Zhang Ruimin. The small factory which was unable to pay its wages was called the Qingdao Daily Appliance Plant, later renamed the Qingdao Refrigerator Plant.

Zhang found Drucker's book, *The Effective Executive* (early 1967 edition) inspirational. One idea in the book deeply touched Zhang, which was Drucker's assertion that 'good management of a factory is always monotonous'. Zhang Ruimin says:

Drucker's words were exactly opposite to the approach we were taking, not only for Haier, at that time, all Chinese enterprises were finding ways to do something exciting every day, for example, engaging in mass campaigns, oath swearing rallies and the like. Drucker's statement was completely different to our approach. But I thought carefully and realized that what he said made sense. Most things in an enterprise should be treated as routine events. Inspired by Drucker, we started doing budgets for Haier, and created the Daily Clearing Act. The act required that 'work for the day should be completed on the day, clean daily and improve standards daily'. The goals for each task were applied for each person every day and were to be finished before the worker left. The clearing daily work method solved the confusion caused by ineffective management, so that the factory, which was near collapse, quickly turned around, and won the first gold medal in the history of Chinese refrigerators.

The refrigerator factory in Qingdao was a starting point. Under the name Haier it is now a world-renowned brand.

Difficult battles

In December 1984, when Zhang Ruimin joined the Qingdao Daily Appliance Plant, the predecessor of today's Haier Group, it was an insolvent neighbourhood factory with only 600 employees. Due to poor management, the company deficit was ¥1.47 million. They were unable to pay wages, and the factory was on the verge of collapse. Since it was a collective enterprise, the state did not give it any money, and the banks were unwilling to do so either, so Zhang Ruimin had to fend for himself. At that time, the main task of leadership was to borrow money to pay the workers' wages. According to one creditor at the time, in order to get the loans for the factory, Zhang Ruimin had to buy drinks for all kinds of creditors.

In addition to having money worries, Zhang Ruimin was also anxious about the people working at the factory. It is very cold in December in the north of China, and the employees had no coal for heating. They had removed the wood from the workshop windows to burn to keep warm, so the plant windows were sealed with plastic film and paper. The workshop was a mess, and the workers were not working, as there was no work to be done.

Sometimes the team heard that certain things would sell, and would quickly produce some items, but as the quality was poor, they could not sell them.

Zhang Ruimin announced the Thirteen Articles to regulate labour discipline at the factory. The list of articles included one stating that staff must not go to the toilet in the workshop. Other provisions included 'no arriving late or leaving early', 'no drinking during working hours', 'smoking is not allowed on the workshop floor, offenders will be fined ¥500 per cigarette'. Another article that left a strong impression on everyone was 'no looting of plant materials'.

The rundown plant of the early 1980s

Zhang has preserved a lot of photos and video materials from the factory as it was in 1984. He joked that at the time he took the pictures, he hoped that if he did not do well with the plant, he could use the photos for verification of how bad it was: 'I would be able to prove that it was such a bad place that I could not be expected to run it well.'

Zhang Ruimin – Thirteen Articles

I did not want to go to Qingdao Daily Appliance Plant but at that time, I was the Home Appliances Company vice manager, and if I did not go, no one else would. I arrived in December 1984 to find 53 requests for transfers. Only a muddy road led to the factory and when it was raining we had to use rope to tie our shoes to our feet or else they got pulled away by the mud.

I thought that even though we had no funds, we could still manage to get the money; there were no products but that would not stop us producing them, what we did really lack was confidence. Developing the business would be very difficult as it was very hard to do anything well. As soon as they heard I wanted to make some changes factory staff showed me a long list of regulations; I did not want so many articles, so we just developed thirteen. The first one was: 'You may not go to the toilet on the workshop floor.' Even this most basic thing was not written anywhere before then. The rest was even more obvious.

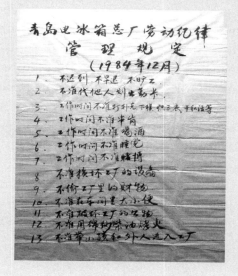

The Thirteen Articles

Leaving the country for the first time

The approach decided on by Zhang Ruimin was to connect his small plant with the German company Liebherr by signing a refrigerator manufacturing technology contract. From October 1984, the Ministry of Light Industry recognized the plant as the last of the fixed production plants.

In that year, for the Liebherr project, Zhang Ruimin left China for the first time. At a German supermarket, he saw no Chinese-made goods. His trip coincided with a local festival; the German person accompanying Zhang pointed up at the fireworks and said: 'Those were imported from your country.' Zhang's blood started to boil when he heard that: would Chinese people always have to rely on the four great inventions of their ancestors?

At this time, Liu Chuanzhi, Lenovo's president wrote about his perceptions of Europe, where he went to study: 'In a supermarket, Italian shoes and those of other countries were placed on the fine shelves, with prices of hundreds of dollars. Chinese shoes were just thrown in a cardboard box, one dollar for one pair. Asians in the United States tended to work for companies engaged in making small, cheap items. In general, there is only one shareholder in those companies, because they do not want to cooperate with others to build anything great.'

After the years of economic backwardness and seclusion, a huge gap between China and the world had emerged. This shocked Zhang and Liu and their sense of grievance drove the business leaders towards entrepreneurship. They separately created ambitious plans to build a Chinese brand.

Zhang Ruimin – German manufacturing

It was very interesting at the time. The approval was granted by the Ministry of Light Industry to introduce a refrigerator production line with an annual output capacity of 50,000 units, I did not dare say this when I went abroad. A production line of 50,000 units per year, what kind of concept was that? In Germany, we made a tour of Siemens, and we saw millions of units under production. In the 1980s when we saw the Siemens factory we were astonished to find that the workshop was accessed by train. The refrigerators followed along the production line, and when complete they went directly into the train cars for transport by rail. This was the line to Hamburg, that was the line to Berlin and so on. At that time, I simply felt that our factory counted for nothing.

After foreign exchange we had just 4.6 million Deutschmarks. I wondered how I could buy the equipment. Later, several pieces of key equipment were introduced, but all the automatic doors were removed. At that time in China we did not use automatic feeding, as it was all done by hand, since we have a lot of people. The imported equipment was just a small part of the process of turning our workshop into a small production line.

My other impression of the Germans was that they were meticulous with regards to quality. Because they had clear processes, if there was even a little defect on a refrigerator on the production line, it was pulled out; even sometimes when I couldn't see the actual flaw, the workers would still take it out. Substandard items were repaired, repolished and then returned to the line.

Another impression I had at that time was that Germany was such an advanced country, but look, what were their workers doing? When I looked inside the factory I saw people who I was told were new workers. What were they doing? They each picked up a clamp, and they were given a piece of steel, and flat file rasps. These were the basic fitter skills I needed when I worked in factories myself. We thought that West Germany was so advanced that they would not need these things. I was told that these technicians were training in all the skills, so that they would have the ability to do whatever was required of them.

Then I compared what I saw in West Germany with what I saw later in Japan. I felt that their quality management really was not the same. The quality management in Japan, including Toyota's Kanban, mainly focused on team organization, the team all worked together, the next step in the process was the next user, and they worked together to improve quality. But although the Germans seemed to be working in a loose way, they were not focused around the team as the centre, it was as if the individual was the centre, and in fact each person's skill level was very high. So the quality of Liebherr products was excellent, even today, I think they are very powerful.

German excellence

You can see how Germany raised the idea of Industry 4.0; every step is very practical. The Japanese people sometimes think that it is not necessary to put so much time into certain things, they believe that as long as they can meet market demand it will be fine. So, that time was very interesting, our model room had a Liebherr refrigerator on one side, and a Japanese refrigerator on the other. The Japanese came and said that the Liebherr refrigerator was good. When Germans came, they said that the Liebherr refrigerator was clumsy, and felt that the Japanese one was more beautiful. One German person was very strong, and as they opened the door to look at the Japanese refrigerator, it bent. He asked how acceptable that was. I saw it and felt the same thing. Then the Japanese came to us and they said, look how strong the German refrigerators are, they are making safes, not refrigerators.

The spirit of entrepreneurship

In 1984, in the era of shortages in China, general domestic house-hold electrical appliance manufacturers had the idea of making a 'quick kill and retreating', by assembling imported parts. In contrast, Haier introduced advanced foreign technology and equipment, and manufactured and sold it itself. The long-term aim was to dominate the market.

Zhang Ruimin decided to introduce refrigerator production equipment from Germany. He developed a 'late start, high starting point' principle in introducing technology. As the leader among the more than 40 businesses introducing foreign refrigerator production technology and equipment, Haier had two marked differences: first, Haier introduced the four-star double-door refrigerator which was not yet on the Asian market; second, while introducing German Haier Liebherr refrigerator production technology and equipment, they also introduced the German DIN (German Institute for Standardization) 1942 standard and ISO international standards.

However, collective enterprises were discriminated against, as they had to travel to Beijing for foreign exchange approval. This was commonly referred to as 'travelling to move forward'. 'When travelling to the train station, we had to pay five fen to buy the tickets, after getting on the train, another ¥2 was spent to rent a stool, then we would sit in the passage between two compartments all the way to Beijing. I had no money to stay in a hotel, so I had to live in hostels. The accommodation was ¥4 per person per day. The bathrooms were open to the sky so we had to take an umbrella with us when we went to the toilet,' remembers Zhang. In the summer of 1985, at a guest house in Jinan, the indoor temperature was 38–40 degrees, and even the ceiling fan was totally useless; Zhang Ruimin and his fellow travellers poured water on the ground to reduce the temperature.

Zhang Ruimin says that encapsulates Haier's entrepreneurial spirit. As a collective enterprise, it had no money to engage in public relations, and did not have any kind of reputation to speak of. Surprisingly, Haier was able to obtain future development opportunities. It was not the background and history of the company and its people that won these opportunities but sheer perseverance. That generation of Haier staff matured with these life experiences.

The Liebherr project required Zhang Ruimin to persuade the Ministry of Light Industry and various provincial departments, and commit to running the project smoothly. Zhang Ruimin promised that he would do the project well, so he had to do it. Eventually, Zhang Ruimin ran the plant himself. The idea was very simple: this was the last chance of survival for the factory, so failure was not an option. At that time, there was no concept of the market economy, as China was still in the planned economy era. Many companies were engaged in various projects, and everyone was busy negotiating foreign technology introduction projects. If contracts were signed, even if a business embarked on a road of reform and opening up, suddenly moving from the closed era into an open one.

Haier's former president Yang Mianmian says:

Introductions sowed the seed. This was the seed for opening up. It prompted us to conduct a series of reforms. Personally, the biggest gain I got from the introduction projects was that before then, I had never seen people working so hard. A general German worker was operating on fruit and vegetable boxes, injection moulded fruit and vegetable boxes. He looked at each box, and what he was doing was inspecting the products, but I saw a certain kind of appreciation in his eyes, an appreciation of the fruits of his labour. After this he worked busily on the machine, so that the next product could be better. This spirit moved me; I suddenly saw that there really were such serious and responsible people in the world. Seeing this shocked my soul to the core. I thought that we should do the same, I wanted to improve myself, and I started serious work. This spirit had a huge impact throughout Haier. I wanted our work to be like theirs, so that each product could be our own work, and we could appreciate it and enjoy what we were doing. So from this starting point as we

*introduced Liebherr technology, we worked very fast, and in that
year completed 10,000 units. We saw immediate benefits.*

Thirty years of Haier

Death or glory

After the signing of the Qingdao Refrigerator Factory and Liebherr technology import contracts on 26 December 1984, the
Chinese side identified three groups of technical personnel to
go to the Liebherr factory for training and study. The first was
scheduled for departure on 12 May 1985.

Chief engineer Yang Mianmian headed the group. There
were three people in charge of the refrigerator product
design, manufacturing processes and product quality testing.
Zhang Ruimin told them:

> *You are all well aware of the current status of our plant;
> we have borrowed money to import this equipment,
> and put it into our refrigerator projects. This is a 'death or
> glory' gamble for the factory. You are going to Liebherr
> for training, carrying the trust of all the factory staff, you
> must conscientiously study the refrigerator manufacturing
> technology taught to you. We want to produce Chinese
> first-class refrigerators as soon as possible.*

Han Zhendong, was part of the group going to Germany. He
joined Haier in 1984, and was serving as Head of Quality Control at the time. He remembers:

> *We were excited but also under huge pressure. Would just
> one month be enough to learn refrigerator manufactur-
> ing technology? We took the train to Beijing to wait for
> visas. We had no fixed residence in Beijing, so we stayed in
> the simple rooms in the basement of the China State Ship-
> building Corporation Hostel. For the whole day, Manager
> Yang took the team through the pre-prepared training*

*programme, breaking it down into great detail, from stan-
dards, design, technology and quality inspection to sheet
metal, powder, absorption, foam, assembly, and testing,
we each had a very clear mandate, so our confidence
increased.*

Zhang Ruimin – Business is people

In the beginning at Haier, workers simply could not do their
jobs; there was no cohesion. The reason we created the Thirteen Articles was that it made things mandatory. In May of my
second year at the factory we started training in Germany.
I nominated those who would go for training, they were all
singled out. After coming back they were all considered technicians, working in the Technology Division. The people who
were selected were very excited to go abroad for training, but
we told everyone that after they came back, they would have
to focus on what they had learned. If they could not learn it,
or if there were any questions, they would have to go back to
being regular workers.

At the time, there were two other companies introducing
Liebherr technology. Including us, that made a total of three
companies. Later on in our relationship, the Liebherr people
told us that they felt that the Chinese people were not all the
same. They said our group of Chinese was not the same as
the other groups. Some of the Chinese students who visited
them just wanted us to go out and see Germany. They felt that
the technology was very simple and that they only needed to
have a quick look at it. When we later merged with a factory in
Wuhan, one of the two mentioned above, we learned that at
that factory, the situation had been different to ours. The choice
of who would go to Germany was based on relationships and

favouritism. Those people were not committed like us; they did not apply themselves to learning. They went to Germany to have a good time. They believed that after coming back from the trip, they could learn as they went along and that the Germans would continue to help them.

But we were not like that. From the very beginning, our attitude was to form a cohesive force. Why do I always say that 'business is people'? Because it really is true. This kind of spirit has an extremely important effect on business. However, even after training the quality of the workers was still very low.

OEC management

Intel's former chairman, Andrew S. Grove, felt that the Chinese have an almost innate creativity when it comes to wealth, but that the operation of their organizations lacked enthusiasm. However, from the beginning Zhang Ruimin's focus was not only on advanced technology, but on finding suitable methods for the management of Chinese enterprises.

Beginning from assembly line management, Zhang learned Taylorism, and created what is known as 'OEC Management'. O stands for Overall, E for Everyone, Everything, Every day, and C for Control and Clear. To summarize, this management ideology means that: 'Everyone does daily tasks on the day, clears their To Do List daily and improves standards daily.'

Zhang Ruimin uses the analogy of a ball on a slope in order to illustrate the need to maintain the market position of the enterprise. The company is under pressure from market competition and any internal staff who are not working optionally, creating an impetus. If there is no braking force, the ball (the enterprise) will roll down the slope. To maintain the position of Haier on the slope (the market), braking is necessary – that is, basic management.

At Haier this is known as 'Haier's Development Law'. Continuing with the analogy of the ball on the slope, OEC management has three levels of deeper meaning:

1. Management is a necessary condition for business success. With no management, there is no braking force, and the ball will slide downwards, so you will not succeed.

2. The focus on management should be to persevere. Management is difficult and painstaking work. Management levels are prone to falling, meaning that even if the brakes are held in place, they will eventually loosen, so they require constant reinforcement. Management is clumsy. There is no way to resolve management issues once and for all. Managers can only work to continually hold the position, repeatedly working on maintenance, only then does the ball stop rolling and stay in place on the slope.

3. Management is dynamic, and endless. As a business moves forward, the braking system should also move up the slope. There is no fixed management style, it needs to be continually adjusted according to corporate objectives, so that it is dynamically optimized as external conditions change. Management styles must not form rigid dogma. Haier's slogan is 'training for the fight, not to watch the fight'. Everything depends on results.

OEC management improves the quality of the people and their output and implementation. Zhang Ruimin often tells employees: 'What is not simple? Being able to do simple things every day is not simple. What is not easy? Things everyone recognizes as very easy, must be done extremely carefully, they are not easy.'

Haier's OEC, like Taylorism, dissected worker actions, the quantification of the task was the basis for assigned targets, quality assessment and incentives. Frederick Winslow Taylor said that he wanted to establish a management system, so that supervisors only needed to respond to exceptions, and did not need to supervise workers, thereby avoiding exhaustion and burnout. Haier used a similar method, using one month on-the-job training to turn newly arrived migrant workers into qualified workers.

At prominent places by the entrance and working areas in the Haier workshop, a red bordered, white 60cm square was painted on the floor, with a pair of green footprints in the centre. This is called the 'Big 6S Footprint'. Standing on the large footprints and looking forward, you will face a sign. The sign says 'finish, straighten, sweep, clean, quality, safety', all of which begin with S in the original Japanese from which the Chinese terms were derived. So this area was referred to as the 6S self-test station. At the daily meetings before work, the heads of the workshops would stand and report on the day's 6S activities. Weak employees would stand on the footprints and reflect on their work.

From December 1998, as the quality of Haier staff improved, the Refrigerator Division promoted the practice of using the 6S footprint up to the level of exchanging best practice, and the other divisions followed. Onsite management, quality management, process improvement and other divisions were invited onto the Big 6S Footprint. The idea of 6S enhanced the enthusiasm of the staff, but the meaning of 6S was then transformed from its original use in reflecting problems to being used to show the optimal method.

6S was a unique way for Haier to strengthen onsite production, intended to allow better utilization of the existing equipment by developing a high level of equipment maintenance and eliminating uneconomic operations (handling, testing, adjusting, etc.). However, the pursuit of excellence in production was not limited to efficiency considerations; the greater purpose was to shape the company's own work ethic. Creating a constructive work ethic in the enterprise took years of trial and nurturing.

The OEC model established the Haier management style: strict, detailed, real, constant. Strict requirements, detailed division of labour, real responsibility, constant perseverance. It not only played a huge role in the development of the enterprise, it also became the basis for the future of Haier process re-engineering.

In 1995 the OEC management model won a state-level enterprise management modernization innovation prize.

Zhang Ruimin – Effective management standards

The biggest problem for Chinese companies was implementing standards and acting on regulatory requirements. Companies might reach them one day, but may not reach them the next. In more sophisticated international enterprises, this problem seemed not to exist. Those enterprises were given a certain set of requirements, and once they were achieved, generally things would not change. But Chinese enterprises are very literal. For example, if I see a dirty workstation and ask a worker to clean it they will do so – that one time. When the workstation gets dirty again the worker will not think to clean it again unless told to do so. Therefore, managers must constantly make demands; we referred to this as 'repeated efforts, making efforts repeatedly'.

For the brand each link is very important, for all staff, for the entire system. If everyone's work is poor, the brand will be poor. Our competition was international brands. Small gaps make large differences. From the product point of view our products may not have differed much from theirs, a little rougher here, not smooth enough there, the difference was not much. But we can see from this small gap that there was a huge difference in management and the quality of our staff.

In his book *The Effective Executive* Peter Drucker said that if the same crisis recurs it is often caused by negligence and laziness on behalf of the managers. This played a huge role in changing my personal management style. At that time, management practice was based around being busy; if a manager worked 10 hours a day, leaving work late, they felt like a good manager. However, Drucker said that excellent managers do not use busy-ness as their standard, their standard is effective management, so they are not dealing with repeated mistakes every day.

In response to this, Haier classified three levels of enterprise management style. Haier's management appraisals were also done according to these three levels. The lowest level of management was a 'steward'; the higher level of management was the 'people manager', and the highest level of management was a 'regime manager'. The stewards followed the well-known Chinese expression 'walls should be made to counter an army, but dams should be made for rivers', meaning that different situations call for different actions and measures should be adopted which are appropriate to the actual situation. In other words, they respond to different situations in different ways. The result would be more management efforts, more complexity and eventually more disorder. 'People managers' are one level higher. They find who is responsible for certain matters, so they are much better than stewards. The most important is the 'regime manager'. Changing the regime can cause the whole enterprise to undergo an orderly development process. As Jim Collins said in *Built to Last*, good company managers are clock builders rather than timekeepers. However, the leadership of many companies like to focus on timekeeping. Whatever timeframe they specify is how long the task should take, but in fact, after building a clock, the time is the time, it cannot be changed by people.

Shattering old ideas: entrepreneur with a hammer

What is the spirit of Haier? Zhang Ruimin says that the spirit involves two guiding forces – the spirit of entrepreneurship and the spirit of innovation. For employees, the spirit of entrepreneurship means that an entrepreneurial approach needs to be maintained at all times. The innovative spirit means always saying yes to user requirements, rather than worrying about Haier's own needs.

One day in 1985, a letter of complaint was received from one particular user who said that the refrigerator he had purchased was defective. Zhang Ruimin inspected the 400 refrigerators in stock in the warehouse, and found that there were 76 refrigerators with various problems. He asked the team to discuss what to do with these refrigerators and two ideas were raised. The first was to fix the problems and sell them cheaply to the workers. At that time the price of a refrigerator for a worker was equivalent to two years worth of food and drink. The other idea was to use them as a public relations tool and send them to relevant government leaders.

Zhang Ruimin said that neither of these was possible, because if they distributed these 76 sub-par refrigerators, tomorrow there would be 760 units, and the day after, there would be 7,600 units. So these flawed refrigerators had to be scrapped. The question then was how. Zhang Ruimin decided that whoever did their job incorrectly, whoever was responsible for making a faulty refrigerator, would personally have to smash it. Faced with the prospect of smashing the products they made with their own hands, many staff were reduced to tears. This situation made a great impact on everyone involved.

Zhang Ruimin and Chief Engineer Yang Mianmian took responsibility, and deductions were made from their wages. Since then, in the appliances industry, Zhang Ruimin has been called the 'entrepreneur with a hammer'.

Zhang Ruimin – The power of concepts

Smashing the refrigerators was a way to solve a particular problem. At that time, Chinese companies were learning from Japanese companies, studying total quality management (TQM). I was very familiar with William Edwards Deming and Joseph M. Juran, who raised the quality of engineering. I did exactly as they said. However, the results were not as good as we wanted. The main reason for this was that the underlying concepts had not been changed. It was not true that all we needed to do was apply total quality management tools. What we really needed was to create a *concept* of total quality management. That was the only way that everyone could really be responsible for the quality of their work, and how everyone could feel that quality was linked to their efforts. To solve this problem and deal with the underlying concepts, we finally adopted a radical approach that made a very strong impact on everyone. What kind of impact? The impact was making them aware that they were responsible for any products or mistakes which they made, because when they picked up that hammer, and smashed their refrigerator, the psychological impact was huge: this product was of their own making, now they were personally smashing it, personally destroying it. For these workers the message was that they should not allow poor quality products to come through their hands in the future.

In fact, it is probably not very well-known to people outside the business that someone reported me for smashing the refrigerators! The Procuratorate came to see me, and asked what right I had to destroy those products. The value of the things we had destroyed was something like ¥400. So, it would have been easy to have said I was a criminal. This issue took up a great deal of my time.

The Procuratorate said that our products were national assets, and that I had no right to destroy them. They said that if the products were flawed, we could always repair them and after repairing them, we could have still sold them. They said there was no need to scrap them. I talked with a deputy of the Procuratorate from the city's Northern District for quite a long time. Finally, I persuaded them to see my reasoning. He said that he understood what I was talking about, and that as long as there was no pressure from above, he would not look into it any further, but that if they did pressure him, I would have to explain the situation once again. After all, that was the time of the Chinese Economic Reform. There were some things which were handled differently under this reform. At that time, it is fair to say that it was very hard to get things done.

Compared to an SOE, not as much care is given to collectives, for example, in making investments and so on. If an SOE loses money, the state will hold you liable, whereas the state does not manage collective enterprises. The Bureau of Light Industry was not able to look after us, meaning we could only depend on our own resources, which is the reason we looked into rural loans. Despite this, we were controlled more than SOEs, as we needed document approval, foreign exchange was hard to arrange, and all raw materials were controlled. When it came to raw materials, the state first gave resources to the large SOEs, then small SOEs, then finally the collective enterprises. The environment was very difficult.

It was also difficult for us to manage the various external relationships, especially the relationships with government figures. Sometimes, if there was a problem with one of these relationships, without being given any reason, we would meet a lot of resistance in our progress, making us likely to stumble. Haier has now developed and become a much bigger company but when we were smaller, if we offended anyone in any of the water, electricity or gas suppliers, even if it was not intentional, for example if we did not go to worship at the right temple, the result would not be good. When we initially started, our yard had no toilet, there was no kind of sewer or septic tank, so we had to dig the toilets manually. No one else would dig them for us, so we had to give people a few packs of cigarettes to do the job. Eventually, the quality of the cigarettes demanded started to increase, and if we gave lower quality ones, people would still not dig for us. Eventually we started using refrigerator tickets, and again, if we did not give out the tickets people would not dig for us. Anyone could strangle our business. This was very difficult.

In retrospect, it was a good thing in a sense. If life is smooth, what can we truly accomplish?

Thirty years of Haier
If I don't go to hell, who will?

Yang Mianmian was born in Wuxi in August 1941, and graduated with a major in Internal Combustion Engines from the Shandong Institute of Technology. She was previously a teacher for the Qingdao Labour Bureau Technical School, a technician for the Qingdao Casting Plant, and Senior Engineer for Qingdao Home Appliances Company. From 1984 to 1993, she served as Deputy Director of the Qingdao Refrigerator Plant.

At the beginning of the 1980s, Yang Mianmian was invited to work with Zhang Ruimin. At that time, the site was almost in ruins. Yang Mianmian once said that, at the time, people felt that moving from offices to factories was like 'going to hell'.

When describing the process of joining the company, Yang Mianmian's description is simple but, in the story of what she has done at Haier, there are a lot of details which reflect her demand for quality and attention to users, as well as her respect for colleagues and entrepreneurial partners. During interviews, Yang Mianmian's language is straightforward and sincere, and co-workers think that with her simple, and even slightly humorous approach, she is good at communicating with employees, helping the company form a consensus in difficult times. 'I concern myself with employees to help them build confidence. As they say in China, women have a softer, more persuasive character,' Yang Mianmian says. 'On the other hand, Chairman Zhang showed a tougher side.'

However, in the early years, it was difficult to see the soft side in Yang Mianmian's own career path. As soon as she arrived at Haier, she took a book called *Refrigerators* from the library. After studying it, she went straight to Shanghai and visited Wujiaochang to find the author, Second Military Medical University professor Shan Dake. It was this visit which led Haier into the field of refrigerator manufacturing. Shan Dake had already had successful experiences with other vendors, and was invited to Qingdao to see the humble factory. He immediately told the team: 'You only need to make refrigerators, soon they will be found on every street, in homes and offices.'

At that time refrigerators were still very much a luxury for Chinese people. Users were very sensitive to the quality of such goods. From day one, Zhang Ruimin and Yang Mianmian's management involved elevating the importance of quality. It is well known that Zhang Ruimin destroyed 76 poor quality refrigerators, what is less known is that on one one occasion Yang Mianmian discovered a hair in the drawer of a refrigerator and seriously investigated to find the responsible employee. Some media reports said that Yang Mianmian's quality requirements for Haier were far stricter than those of its Chinese competitors. In an interview she revealed that Haier's imagined adversary was actually their partner – Germany's Liebherr.

When Haier introduced equipment from Liebherr and began

a seven-year cooperation with the company, Yang Mianmian and colleagues visited Germany. The Chinese team was so focused that the German workers referred to them as 'ideological people'. These ideological people applied a great deal of pressure to the German team. For the exteriors of the refrigerators, Yang Mianmian, despite the advice from people around her of the refrigerators, did not use paint, instead she insisted on powder coating, which reflected the latest technology. As a technology provider, Liebherr itself had no experience in this area, so it had to build its own equipment and learn how to use it, then they passed this on to Haier. At that time, some domestic rivals were travelling all over the world to procure the most advanced parts, whereas Haier let the German side take care of their production capacity.

After the start of production, Haier also requested that Liebherr sell 20,000 made-in-China refrigerators in Germany so that, through the strict requirements of German users, they could ensure the suppliers unreservedly passed on their best technology. The refrigerator called the Blue Line has now become a part of appliance history. The high evaluations of German users were recorded in German professional journals. What is surprising is that these tests show that the quality of Haier products exceeded that of their teacher, Liebherr.

In order to surpass the quality of the widely used Japanese technology, Yang Mianmian personally learned the difference between four-star refrigerators and three-star refrigerators. After returning to China, she compared the crystallization within three and four-star refrigerators, and made photographic records of the freezing process. At the laboratory of the Second Military Medical University she learned that the rapid freezing in four-star refrigerators was capable of generating small crystals, which, when thawed, would not pierce the cell membranes of the food and cause fluid outflow, unlike the larger crystals generated in three-star refrigerators.

This was why the flavour was preserved by the higher-grade refrigerators. 'When we talk about "keeping food fresh", that was the mechanism behind it,' Yang Mianmian explained. Subsequently, Haier produced Asia's first four-star refrigerators, ahead of Sharp and other Japanese manufacturers.

Many successful entrepreneurs are somewhat paranoid, even tending to look for problems where none exist. As Chinese business culture began the transition from interpersonal relationships towards reputation-based trust the quality of Haier refrigerators met certain requirements and the Haier management team began to look for ways to authenticate their products. This would allow them to create a good reputation for the products and the brand. Yang Mianmian remembers the day Zhang Ruimin first talked about introducing the new ISO 9001 standard he had read about in a newspaper. She formed a plan, and visited Shanghai once again, to go to Det Norske Veritas (DNV). Founded in 1864 and headquartered in Oslo, Norway, DNV is an independent foundation, providing risk management services. At that time, there were more than twenty industrial countries which recognize DNV Management System certification. Its services include traditional ISO 9000 certification through to QS 9000 certification. DNV had only just arrived in China and had only three staff members in the country. After receiving Yang Mianmian's request they readily agreed to give guidance and help Haier.

In 1992, Haier was granted the ISO 9001 international quality system certification, becoming a qualified world-class supplier. It was the first Chinese household electrical appliance enterprise to obtain the certification. When asked whether Haier had worldwide ambitions at the time, Yang Mianmian thought for a while, and then answered frankly that the idea she and Zhang Ruimin had was simply to prove the quality of Haier refrigerators, in order to show that the German technical level had been completely transferred into Haier's own hands.

Quality comes first

Peter Drucker said: 'The purpose of business is to create and keep a customer.' In line with this, from the beginning, Haier established the concept of creating customer value.

Zhang Ruimin explains:

> In practice, I found Drucker's idea of creating customers very helpful. Many Chinese companies attempted to go where there was a profit. However, Drucker believed that yields are not the goal of an organization's business activities, but are a limiting factor. In actual operations, as the leader of an enterprise, it is easy to look for profit margins.
>
> Soon after we started, China was still an economy facing shortages, and all products were in short supply. As long as you made products, you could sell them, so businesses were rushing to make the goods. With production came sales, and with sales came huge profits. Many companies rushed to capitalize on this situation., but we realized that profit-making is not the goal of an enterprise. Focusing only on high profits would not have been enough to guarantee our future survival. Instead, we focused on quality, so it seemed we made a lot less profit. Some of our competitors were producing almost a million units, whereas we produced less than 100,000 units. However, as the supply-demand relationship changed, many businesses closed down overnight, while we had a stable foothold. This confirmed to me that creating customers is the soul of a business.

After smashing those refrigerators, Zhang Ruimin and Yang Mianmian implemented a triple inspection system (self-inspection, mutual inspection, special inspection) for production process quality control. Making sure that employees understood the 'defective product = waste' concept, and carrying out quality team activities, broke the company away from the idea of small-scale production. The relationship between yield and quality, was balanced by making quality the prime consideration.

In 1985, Haier launched the first generation of four-star

refrigerators, 'Qindao-Liebherr'. The refrigerator market was entering a phase of explosive growth, and Haier's product won over the country, selling in all major cities. Because there was a big refrigerator market supply and demand gap, prices continually increased. In October 1986 Zhang Ruimin organized a whole factory discussion to look at what to do if, after two years, the market softened, or stagnated. The conclusion was that blindly increasing production would eventually lead to the loss of the market. After this discussion Haier held back on expanding production and instead focused on providing better products.

Haier's development goal was to establish a good reputation with consumers. When users wanted to buy a refrigerator, their first thought should be 'Qingdao-Liebherr'. In December 1988, Haier won the gold medal at the first national quality assessment for the industry.

The weak market arrived as scheduled. If 1984 to 1988 was the first phase of the implementation of Haier's brand strategy, then from 1989 to 1991, Haier entered its strategic second phase. At this time, as the quantity of commodities began to meet demand, the gap between supply and demand started to slow, so quality, service and price gradually became key parts of market demand. In addition, macro-control and administrative measures affected the market, weak demand began to emerge, and consumers began to select products based on quality and variety. Due to its initial steps, Haier was easily able to cope with changes in the market. In 1989, as domestic prices plummeted, Haier saw a 12 per cent price increase, and its products were still in short supply. The quality-driven strategy had begun to bear fruit. In 1990, Haier was awarded the Golden Horse and National Quality Management Award by national authorities.

To improve quality Haier emulated GE and implemented Six Sigma management. Sigma is a statistical unit which represents the standard deviation from the mean. It can be used to measure the degree of perfection of a process, specifically to see how many times mistakes are made per million operations. Six Sigma Management identifies and eliminates defects caused by processes to improve product quality, minimizing the changes made to production and commercial workflows. Achieving Six Sigma means that in the production of products, 99.99966 per cent of the output has no quality problems (3.4 defects per 1 million). Haier implemented Six Sigma management to ensure that there was a whole company consensus in production – even if product failure rates were just one in a thousand, for one particular user, that would be 100 per cent. Haier's objective was that every process, every product and every service experienced by the user was near-perfect.

Haier refrigerators win the first gold medal in the history of China

First create brand teams, then create branded products

Kōnosuke Matsushita once said that business success depends on people – if there are no people there will be no business. Similarly, Jack Welch said that GE was in the business of making great people, and then those great people were making great products and services.

When talking about Matsushita and Welch's management philosophy, Zhang Ruimin said: 'Human resources are fundamental to the success of Haier. What is a business? In the final analysis it is just a group of people. What is management? In the final analysis it is just leveraging the talents of people. If you can collect the power of a lot of people together, the business will be successful. If the staff are willing to lend me their strength to achieve our shared goals, this is successful management.'

The goal of Haier was to create a world famous brand, and to bring about this goal of becoming a world famous brand, the company needed to shape people who were able to build a world famous brand. To this end, Haier established the 'first make the people, then create the brand' concept of staff recruitment, implementing the management precept that 'employees should be controlled using promotion based on competition, rotating after completion, with the laggers being dismissed.'

More than a decade after the Panasonic management philosophy came to China, Panasonic representatives visited Haier. They looked at the neat and orderly production site, and the fully engrossed attitude of the workers, they saw the detailed statistical tables, staff suggestion boxes, slogans and so on and they were hugely surprised. One commented, 'When we saw your production line, it felt like seeing Panasonic 30 years ago, it was vibrant, and full of life. Seeing Zhang Ruimin is just like seeing China's own Mr Matsushita. It is really a pleasure.'

Thirty years of Haier

The great value of micro-innovations

The seventh year of the Haier venture was 1991, and at the commemorative meeting, Zhang Ruimin announced a new technical innovation: the Qiming welding torch.

'This was announced by CEO Zhang himself, originally I did not dare think about it, as I could not believe that an innovation would actually be named after me,' Li Qiming said. He was a senior employee at Haier, mainly as a technician.

Around 1990, in order to improve production efficiency, Haier encouraged all employees to engage in work-related innovation. Problems could be raised immediately with the goal of finding a solution to them, innovators were rewarded, and everyone's enthusiasm was very high. It was a most difficult time for Haier, but the entire factory was full of energy.

As a workshop director, Li Qiming was working on the production line every single day, pondering how to solve some of the production bottleneck issues. 'Welding was an important step in the process, as many parts on the refrigerator needed to be welded. If not handled properly, welding problems would directly affect the refrigerator's cooling ability.'

Li Qiming still remembers: 'We were using the smallest torches in China, size three. The head was about 7–8cm, and the flame reached up to 15cm, with a welding temperature of 1500°C. There were seven or eight conduits in the refrigerator, and welds had to be made around them, this was very inconvenient, not only affecting the quality of welding and production rhythm, but worse, the sides of the products were often burned and damaged. We had no choice but to add an asbestos block retaining plate to the welding station.'

Li Qiming thought that it would be better if the torch could be a size smaller. At that time domestic refrigerator industry production had just started, and there were no special welding torches. Li Qiming carefully studied the welding process used in the production of household refrigerators, and began to transform the torch. 'After several tests, I changed the angle of the torch head from the original 120 degrees to 90 degrees, and shortened the length of the torch head by half; the torch head aperture was also reduced by 0.3mm. After this transformation, the flame of the new torch was shortened by 8cm, the temperature could be controlled at 800°C –1000°C, and the original problems were resolved.'

The Qiming torch improved both the welding process and production efficiency. Subsequently, Haier created a wave of technological innovations with many workers even using their own time to perform some of the necessary research. During this period, a lot of innovations named after employees emerged: The Xiaoling wrench, the Yunyan mirror and Shenqiang hooks, among others. In 1998 alone, Haier employees made 37,000 rationalization proposals, and 19,000 were adopted, worth ¥113 million in economic returns.

Li Qiming repeatedly stresses that the most important factors for the invention of the Qiming torch were Haier's relaxed environment for innovation, and employees being given the right guidance. 'At that time, most of the employees had been at the company for a long time, and their education level was not high. After arriving at Haier, CEO Zhang promised to lead us out of the woods, and that he would introduce a four-star standard production line from West Germany. He had a lot of determination, so the employees saw hope, and they agreed to stay at the company.

'In August 1988, we were sent to study in West Germany, and build a second refrigerator production line. CEO Zhang went to the train station to see us off, and he said to me, "Qiming, work hard." I faithfully held those instructions in my heart, and whatever job I did later on, I maintained the attitude of innovation.'

Li Qiming has left the assembly line and now works in the Haier Computer Aftermarket Division.

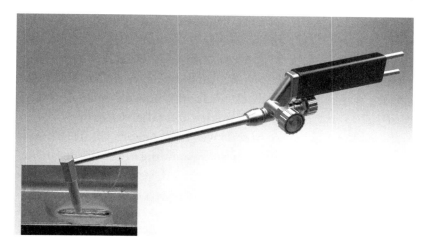

The Qiming welding torch: internal innovation at work

The birth of a brand

In 1985 Haier created its brand name, and came up with its distinctive brand concept – strive to be the best. In order to make the company stand out in the fiercely competitive appliance industry, Haier initially relied on the quality of the brand. When other home appliance enterprises began to focus on product quality, Haier's focus shifted to service.

In terms of products and services, Haier had conceptual differences from other companies. It was interested in providing pre-sales service as well as post-sales service and believed that service should include not only maintenance, installation, queries, and so on, but also an understanding of the views and needs of consumers, enabling better development and modification of products. The user's troubles became Haier's problems. This approach led to Haier developing new products to meet the needs of potential users, thus creating a new market.

During the transition to services, Haier worked on the basis that the 'user is always right'. Starting from this awareness, it further introduced the 'good faith forever' service concept and 'international star service' one-stop, comprehensive service commitment, meaning that the Haier brand formed a family-like relationship with its users. 'Star Service' strives to deliver as many services as the customer needs. And because Haier wanted to ensure complete customer satisfaction, the company developed a closed loop service system with feedback, including internal pre-sales, sales, post-sales service, telephone service and other services.

Since the concept of brands was then new to China, Chinese enterprises had a very limited understanding of the deeper meaning of brands and there were many prejudices about branding. But Haier had realized earlier than many others that the brand refers to the *relationship* between businesses and their customers. This means that the brand management process, in the final analysis, is about delivering a commitment to consumers and society. The Haier brand is a commitment to consumers, first that the company will continue to satisfy the users' unexpected requirements and second that the company ensures consumers are able to use Haier products without complaint.

During the brand strategy phase (1984 to 1991), Haier spent seven years dedicated to making refrigerator products. At this stage, it Haier established a comprehensive quality management system, the main purpose of which was to improve quality, and enhance the core competitiveness of the enterprise. Then, to make the change from being product-driven to brand-driven, long-term investment was made in the brand, to accumulate brand equity, and enhance brand value.

In order to ensure that the Haier brand did not slip, Zhang Ruimin made it clear that Haier was not competing based on price, rather they were fighting over value. In the war of value, the ultimate goal was to meet the individual needs of consumers.

Zhang Ruimin – The brand is the real asset

Many Chinese companies are primarily OEMs (Original Equipment Manufacturers – companies that make a part or subsystem that is used in another company's end product), but we wanted to have our own brand because a lot of profits in OEM are taken by the middlemen. So we had to build our own brand. Many people give up when they see risks, whereas I think we should welcome the risks, looking for opportunities to succeed.

I think that all assets should be seen as liabilities. Only the brand is the true asset. If you say that the plant, fixed assets, and production lines are all world class, but you do not have a brand, if you do OEM for people, tomorrow people will find cheaper alternatives, so your assets become downright liabilities. Someone once said that in the Information Age software is everything, and hardware is nothing. It sounds very strange, but that really is the case.

The brand concept that Haier wanted to create was: the user is always right. But because the user's requirements are being continually revised we must constantly improve quality in all areas in order to maintain or enhance the value of the brand. We must meet the growing requirements of the user so that they continue to receive satisfactory service.

Self-management

Peter Drucker said that traditional managers used to have subordinates, now they have outcomes. Zhang Ruimin, who took Drucker as his spiritual mentor, injected the 'management innovation' gene into the company during the infancy of Haier. Haier was one of the first Chinese enterprises to implement a 'self-managed team', and this was very important in the future management of Haier, laying a good foundation for the organization.

Drucker pointed out that in improving industrial efficiency, Frederick Taylor's motivation was not to create profits for owners but to benefit the workers. Taylor's main motivation was to create a new type of society. In this society, owners and workers, capitalists and proletarians would all have common interests in productivity, so a harmonious working relationship could be established. Zhang Ruimin also managed the implementation of Taylorism at Haier, looking under the surface of Taylorism, he gained deep insight into its true meaning.

Haier's management, especially its on-site management, was very strict, but Zhang knew that business success does not depend on strict management systems, but on the sense of participation and self-management of all employees. Staff without self control and self-management are not good staff, and enterprises which lack self control and self-management are by no means good enterprises. Zhang Ruimin wanted to train staff to be fully conscious, believing that unconscious staff behaviour often leads to failure.

Haier's self-management started with pre-shift meetings at the workshop in 1990. The purpose of the meetings was to solve production problems such as quality, production balancing, equipment management, usage of materials, etc. The meetings allowed employees to manage themselves, and to receive the management of their team.

On the basis of the pre-shift meetings, Haier started self-managing team activities. The aim was to put the pressure of production targets directly onto the members of the teams. Each team was given its own tasks, and was responsible for the inventory, materials planning, personnel arrangements, production targets, product cost targets and product quality. Staff no longer worked mechanically with little or no thought but began to assume a wider range of responsibilities. This model meant there was no direct staff supervision, as monitoring and evaluation were conducted by a team of employees. Employees formed relationships of mutual respect, and they had to learn to communicate, criticize, and offer mutual instruction as well as improve as individuals.

By empowering staff in this way, trust was also created between management and workers. Managers lost little power or control, because they could fully utilize the ideas of all the workers, rather than only those of the managers, who were fewer in number. In other words, they were able to enjoy even more power than before.

The environment of mutual cooperation impacted strongly on the behaviour of employees. Leadership became less important as there was a transition from *instructive* management to *guidance* management. Managerial roles were adjusted from controlling the core functions to creating a protective and supportive environment, motivating employees to acquire knowledge and skills, and developing their willingness and capacity to accept and manage risks. Such leadership is indirect, latent and invisible. When indirect leadership is performed in the best possible way, employees say: 'We achieved this ourselves.' This kind of organization is what management theorists call the 'learning organization'.

In 1998, Haier began 'to work on studies, and turn studies into work' through the creation of interactive learning teams. The first aspect of Haier's learning approach was the important word 'interactive'. Zhang Ruimin pointed out that interaction is based on the needs of the situation and also the needs of the competitive market:

Ten years ago we could not have done this because at that time, management was in a state of total chaos, and the quality of personnel was far lower than it is now. At that point we had to manage with a strict regime, and employees just had to passively accept it. Now, Haier employees have moved from passive acceptance to self-management, strict management systems alone were not able to push employees to offer more of themselves.

At the same time, market competition also requires interaction. Under the planned economy the quality of the business had no direct connection with the individuals, whereas, under the market economy, personal interests were directly tied to corporate risks. In addition, Haier's goal was to enter the world top 500, creating a famous global brand for China. Only if all Haier employees agreed to this goal, could employees work together harmoniously to achieve the common objective. Without interaction it is impossible to achieve the set goals.

The second important aspect of the interactive learning team is the concept of the 'team'. The business intelligence of a team does not equal the sum of the IQs of the team members. Haier was team learning as the way to solve this issue.

Team learning is a skill. A team of talented learners may not be able to become a learning team just as a group of talented athletes may not become a sports team capable of outstanding achievements. In a learning team everyone learns how to learn together.

Zhang Ruimin proposed a formula: Creative kinetic energy = Staff (the number of employees dedicated to improving the business results) × speed (the speed that results can be realized and new initiatives can be formed). He explains this formula in this way:

The kinetic energy of an enterprise is formed by multiplying these two factors, if either is missing or low, then it will not work. Therefore, management should adhere to the people-oriented principle, better approaches and ideas required the agreement of employees and the employees' initiatives are the best guarantee of the execution of those ideas.

Only if a small interactive learning team could be built for every shift, every workshop and every factory would Haier become a large interactive learning organization. Only if each employee, shift and workshop was able to grow, could the competitiveness of the entire enterprise grow, and only then could the desired growth be achieved.

Zhang Ruimin says about self-management: 'I always think of Theodore Levitt's words, "An organization's mission is to allow ordinary people to do extraordinary things." Haier hopes to become such an organization.'

Thirty years of Haier

Shi Chunjie – Everyone is responsible

Shi Chunjie worked in Haier's Quality Inspection Department from 1989. He says that the most important task of the department is to carry out checks on products, and not to miss any flaws. 'Sometimes there is a tension between quality and yield. However, Haier focused on quality, even if it affected the yield,' Shi Chunjie says.

Shi Chunjie remembers that at one point they found that there was a small gap between the refrigerator door seal and cabinet, so small that only professionals could see it, and it did not affect the quality of the refrigeration, but even this small gap meant that the product did not pass quality inspection. They had to stop the production on the door assembly line, which meant they had to shut the entire plant down. At that time, there was a high demand for refrigerators, and stopping production for a day would lead to a great loss.

Then, Zhang Ruimin came to the workshop to see the production; he saw Shi Chunjie and asked: 'When can we resume work?'

In fact, Shi Chunjie was hoping that Zhang Ruimin would tell him to start the production line but he did not, he gave the decision-making power to the Quality Inspection Department. In terms of quality, Haier gave veto power to Quality Inspection. 'The whole plant was mobilized to solve the problem; finally on the third afternoon, the refrigerator door seal was repaired, and only then could they resume production,' says Shi Chunjie.

In the 1980s, there was no quality management system for Chinese-made products. To ensure the quality of Haier refrigerators the company established a comprehensive quality management system, formed of a self-inspection, mutual inspection, and special inspection regime. Staff on each shift performed quality inspection checks and a strict, meticulous professional examination was given to products as they came off the line. Because there were special inspectors, employees developed a sense of dependency, and the rework rate for products was relatively high. This was not only inefficient but could also easily lead to defective products slipping through the net. In view of this situation, Zhang Ruimin proposed creating a special team outside the shifts.

The inspection team did not have dedicated quality inspectors, the products made by employees were instead subject to self and mutual inspection, the wages originally given to the quality inspector were taken and divided among all the members of the team. In this way, not only was the quality of products enhanced, but productivity increased and shift team member responsibility and cohesion were created.

After special inspectors were eliminated, the staff within shifts not only started carefully examining products made during their own shift, they also conducted a second inspection on the products produced by the previous station. In the whole team, everyone became a quality inspector, and everyone was responsible for product quality.

After the creation of self-management shifts, shifts were reduced in size from the original eight members to seven people, however, the product qualification rate reached 100 per cent. The most important thing to note was that these seven individuals shared the income of eight people; the self-managed teams became totally autonomous.

Shi Chunjie has strong feelings about the system: 'After the creation of self-management shifts, consciousness and self-discipline was very high. Under the premise of good management of their own tasks, and with mutual supervision, the self-managed teams improved the quality and efficiency of the entire production process.'

With such a strong sense of quality, Haier Group took seven

years to create a stable quality and management system for future rapid development. In the final analysis, the only reason that Haier was able to do this was that the enterprise gave free rein to the respect and passion of their employees.

Shi Chunjie said:

CEO Zhang's management has always been people-oriented, focused on management with the minimum actions, following the Chinese Daoist term of 'taking action by taking no action'. From the self-management teams of the 1980s, to the Strategic Business Unit (SBU) of the 1990s, to the micro-enterprises of today, in the last 30 years, Haier has always been people-oriented, and aimed at maximizing people's independence and creativity.

Zhang Ruimin in a workshop

Haier's diversification (1992–1998)

3

Bolder, faster – Deng Xiaoping's southern tour

In the 1980s a struggle was raging between the proponents of capitalism and the proponents of socialism. Special Administrative Zones, rural contracting, securities, private enterprises, and foreign-funded enterprises were all ways to handle the market economy, but each of them had been the focus of ideological disputes. At the beginning of the 1980s, a citizen could buy eggs for five fen from the market, and then sell them to their neighbour for six fen, but in doing so risked being labelled a speculator. In fact, speculation was considered a crime until 1997.

Opening up was not easy. In 1987, after the implementation of a planned commodity economy, the Thirteenth Party Congress proposed 'the organic unity of plan and market'. However, the report of the Thirteenth Congress was still denied by some dogmatists, and there was a resurgence of the planned economy from 1989 to 1991. In 1990, changes occurred in Eastern Europe. Soon after this, the Soviet Union dissolved, and some people raised questions about China's reform and opening up.

It was in this context that the 88-year-old Deng Xiaoping visited the south, from 18 January to 21 February 1992. He ended the ideological struggle with a speech he gave during his visit, which included the phrase 'we should have a little more courage, the pace should be a little faster'. This became a slogan for popular reform.

Deng Xiaoping's general idea was that China should be bold in trying new things, because 'if we spend all our time debating, nothing will get done.'

Deng Xiaoping explicitly gave the 'three benefits' criteria:

The reason some people hesitate to carry out the reform and opening up policy and dare not break new ground is, in essence, that they are afraid it would mean introducing too many elements of capitalism and, indeed, taking the capitalist road. The crux of the matter is whether the road should be capitalist or socialist. The judging criteria are mainly to see whether productivity will be conducive to the development of a socialist society, whether it will help enhance the overall strength of a socialist country, and whether it will help to improve people's living standards.

Market economy

In October 1992, the fourteenth CPC National Congress report proposed that China 'start a new revolution', that is, the transition from a planned economy to a socialist market economy.

When the words 'market economy' were published, Chinese GATT negotiations chief Long Yuantu breathed a sigh of relief, as he no longer had to worry about what vocabulary he would need to use to talk to foreigners about China's economic system: 'In fact, we took only six years to solve the problem; the solution was recognizing that China was a market economy.'

From 1989 to 1991, China's annual GDP growth rate was only about 5 per cent, and in 1992, when the market economy was proposed, it rose to 12.8 per cent.

That year, at the Third Plenary Session of the Fourteenth People's Congress, the CPC Central Committee Decision on Some

Issues Regarding the Establishment of a Socialist Market Economic System was passed. After the meeting, China's economic reform began to develop. From 1993 to 1998, China implemented a number of reforms in the areas of finance, taxation, foreign trade, foreign exchange, investment, pricing, distribution, real estate and social security, clarifying the direction of reform of the enterprise system. It laid a solid foundation for the movement of the economy towards the market. The market began to play a fundamental role in resource allocation, and the price of most products and services started being regulated by the market.

Birth of the stock market

On 26 November 1990, the Shanghai Stock Exchange was formally established and began operations on 19 December. This was the first stock exchange in mainland China since the founding of the new country.

The Chinese government hoped to show the world that China's reformed market doors would not be closed to them. Shanghai mayor Zhu Rongji spoke at the opening ceremony of the Shanghai Stock Exchange. He began his speech by saying: 'This shows that China will continue to unswervingly pursue the reform and opening up policy.'

Shenzhen started preparations almost at the same time as the Shanghai Stock Exchange, but was only formally approved by the People's Bank of China on 11 April 1991, after a trial of more than five months. Shenzhen Stock Exchange finally held a formal opening ceremony on 3 July 1991.

The evolution of the Chinese new financial order concealed an economic and political power struggle between two different factions. After visiting the Shenzhen Stock Exchange on his southern tour, Deng Xiaoping pointed out that some people still insisted that stocks were a capitalist product. He believed: 'The planned economy is not equivalent to socialism, as capitalism also has plans; the market economy is not capitalism, as socialism also has markets. Planning and markets are economic tools.' After the pilots were completed in Shanghai and Shenzhen, the results confirmed the success of the projects. Therefore, socialism could draw on some of the useful aspects of capitalism.

The new generation of entrepreneurs

The year 1992 was a turning point in the growth of Chinese entrepreneurship. In May of that year, the State Economic Reform Commission issued Provisional Regulations of Limited Liability Companies, and Provisional Regulations on Share Limited Companies. A large number of government agencies, research institutes and intellectuals were inspired by the Deng Xiaoping southern tour speech and took the initiative to venture 'into the sea' as the Chinese say, and create their own businesses. The Class of 92, as they were called, included Yu Minhong, Chen Dongsheng, Tian Yuan, Hu Bosen, Guo Fansheng, Feng Lun, Wang Gongquan, Pan Shiyi, Yi Xiaodi, Wu Kegang, and Zhu Xinli. They were the ones who tested the waters of the Chinese modern enterprise system, and were the first Chinese entrepreneurs to have a clear, unambiguous shareholder consciousness.

In the 1980s, the main risks faced by entrepreneurs were institutional ones, while the market risk was small. In the 1990s, the years of growth, entrepreneurs had to face double risks – dealing with both institutions and the market. Because of the double risk, many of the companies that initially appeared successful did not survive and many of the then all-powerful entrepreneurs are now unknown.

In this exciting year, 'let's all jump into the sea' became the catch phrase of the times. Author Ling Zhijun described the scene:

Almost all of the bans had been revoked. The government could make a company, schools could make a profit, teachers could work part-time, officials could do business, people could legally profit from reselling tight supplies. One provincial procuratorial organ publicly stated that: 'rebates, commissions income and part-time income would not be legally pursued'. The industry and commerce department of another province subsequently announced that anyone who would like to run a company did not have to apply for a business license, and did not have to pay management fees ...

In 2008, Bao Xiaodong wrote in his article '1992: Deng Xiaoping's Southern Tour gives birth to the "Class of 92 Entrepreneurs"' for *Southern Metropolitan News*:

The Class of '92 were the group who really injected commercial value into mainstream values of Chinese society; many mainstream elites jumped into the sea creating a new chapter in the development of modern enterprises and economic change. The media of the nineties recorded that era honestly and passionately. Even now, if you go to China's most remote villages you can see advertisements on the walls which were the invention of that time. Around then many dazzling enterprises and entrepreneurs were born. They focused on marketing and even used Mao Zedong thoughts for corporate governance. The list includes famous companies like Aiduo, Qinchi, Taiyangshen, Giant and so on, but many rapidly declined shortly afterwards.

The focus of this generation of entrepreneurs was property rights. In the early 1980s, Professor Li Yining, who raised the idea of stock reform, asserted that 'the success of China's economic reform depends on ownership reform.' In 1993, the CPC Central Committee Decision on Some Issues Regarding the Establishment of a Socialist Market Economic System offered property rights reform and enterprise system innovation to establish a foundation for the new idea of the market economy. The basic characteristic of the modern enterprise system can be summed up as clear property rights, clear responsibilities, separation of enterprise and government, and scientific management.

Liu Chuanzhi, who thrived during this period, was one of the lucky entrepreneurs who successfully navigated the teething problems of the new market economy. In 1994, in order to avoid ownership issues constraining enterprise development, the

Chinese Academy of Sciences, the major shareholder of Lenovo, came up with the idea of transferring 35 per cent of its assets to Lenovo. This was a pilot for the sharing of dividends. In 1998, Lenovo changed its name to the Lenovo Group (Holdings) Company. At the same time, the plan to transfer the dividends held by Lenovo employees into equity came into effect. Lenovo's property reform became a standard for the reform of SOEs.

The Provisional Regulations of Limited Liability Companies, and Provisional Regulations on Share Limited Companies clarified property ownership. One aspect of this was that it allowed private enterprises to flourish; another was that it gradually became the direction of SOE reform.

In 1997, as the new century approached, the country was full of small and medium SOEs with excessive competition, but through processes such as closing, suspending, merging and transferring, invigorating large enterprises while relaxing control over small ones, restructuring and reorganization the market eliminated them. This market reform – which is the essential attribute of privatization – was tragic for the 50 million employees of state enterprises who faced the hardship of finding new employment, but after several rounds of pain, the final batch of enterprises achieved a 'soft landing'.

China connected with the world

In the final decade of the twentieth century the information revolution began.

In September 1994, China's Directorate General of Telecommunications of the Ministry of Posts and Telecommunications of China signed a bilateral agreement on the Internet with the US Department of Commerce. The Directorate General of Telecommunications stipulated in the agreement that the American company Sprint would open two dedicated 64K lines (one in Beijing, the other in Shanghai). China was finally connected with the world.

In May of that year, China Telecom officially opened China's largest, fastest public computer network, Chinanet, with the most extensive coverage and most users nationwide; its physical nodes covered more than 200 cities in 30 provinces, municipalities and autonomous regions.

A group of young Chinese entrepreneurs realized the potential of the Internet. In 1996, Zhang Shuxin founded Information Highway Communications Limited, and this became mainland China's first service provider for the Internet. Later in the year, at MIT, Zhang Chaoyang, borrowed $225,000 from two MIT professors, one of them Nicholas Negroponte, and in February 1998 founded Sohu – even the name was 'influenced by' that of Yahoo. At the same time, Netease and Sina were also set up, and a balance of forces between the three major portals in China began to emerge. In November 1998, Tencent was founded, becoming the first Chinese Internet instant messaging software developer.

In 1998, venture capital entered China and Internet entrepreneurs sprang up soon after. Sequoia Capital China Founding Managing Partner, Neil Shen recalled: 'Needless to say the Internet created Chinese venture capital.' Sequoia Capital's internal statistics show that about 70 per cent of the profits of China's venture capital industry were accounted for by the Internet.

Says Neil Shen: 'I feel that the very important point is that the Internet has always been a very interesting market in the Chinese economy. Access to the industry is relatively relaxed and low, so for the vast majority of entrepreneurs, as long as you have an idea, and the support of a small amount of funds, you can enter the industry.'

With the support of venture capital, a large number of Chinese Internet companies were subsequently listed overseas. Options were used to recognize the contributions of various entrepreneurs to a business. The value and spirit of the new entrepreneurs depends on their reliability, so as they begin to accumulate capital, the concept of having a founder becomes important. Internet entrepreneurs became innocent millionaires. They were unencumbered by the historically negative connotations of money-making in China.

Thirty years of Haier

Unconventional development

When talking about the survival of enterprises, Zhang Ruimin notes, 'There are no successful enterprises, only enterprises which keep up with the times.' Haier's key development moments confirm this saying, since Haier really followed the rhythm of the times.

From 1991 to 1993, Haier went through a phase of extraordinary development. It captured the historical opportunity given by the country's macroeconomic expansion, making its first attempt to diversify its range of white goods. With the support of Qingdao municipality government, Haier merged with Qingdao Freezer and Air Conditioner Plants, and the new group was established on 20 December 1991.

When the Chairman and Managing Director Zhang Ruimin talked about the Group's development direction during the inaugural meeting, he said: 'First we have to strive for the sound development of economies of scale in the shortest possible time, and make a foothold in the domestic market, so we can be China's home appliance industry's leading group, thereby strengthening production, quality and variety. At the same time, we will actively develop our export strategy and target overseas markets. Expanding the export volumes and types of export, and occupying more of the world market is not enough, so we will set up production plants abroad, to facilitate our operations in the international market. This will allow us not only to expand the scope and scale of the existing overseas institutions, but also gradually to develop towards becoming a truly transnational corporation, so that we can participate more easily in international competition, as we strive to become a world-famous brand.'

Zhang Ruimin's idea was bold, particularly with regards to aiming for both the domestic and foreign markets. But, two months after that, Deng Xiaoping's southern tour lectures gave Haier even greater confidence.

In this new-found spirit of optimism, the company expanded the scale of production. In June 1992, Haier decided to borrow money to lease a few acres of land in the Tech Development Zone in Qingdao, creating the largest home appliance industrial park in China at that time.

On 23 September 1992, Haier began issuing the first batch of corporate financing bonds and raised ¥30 million for the construction of Haier Industrial Park. On 19 November 1993, Haier listed on the stock market, and the funds raised reached ¥300 million. Using modern means of raising capital, Haier transformed from a conventional refrigerator factory into an enterprise with significant production and operating scale.

Hongxing Electrical Factory merger ceremony

Activating shocked fish

During the 1990s, in order to survive in the increasingly open and competitive market, Chinese companies focused on technology development and quality control, putting great effort into service, product image and so on. The result was that a number of domestic brands were gradually established that consumers felt comfortable buying.

At the same time, multinational companies began entering China. China's actual utilized foreign investment soared from $10.3 billion in 1995 to $48.1 billion in 1995. With international competition coming into China, as soon as the products made by domestic enterprises left the factory they were in fact entering an international market. Domestic enterprise technology was low level, product quality was poor, and competitiveness was weak. Coupled with market segmentation, and the narrowing of the existing market space, this led to excessive market competition.

Under these circumstances, brand reputation became an intangible asset of the business, and the intangible content of outstanding domestic brands greatly increased. After becoming China's number one brand for appliances, Haier discovered that they could use their brand as a core tool, and carry out restructuring, so that they could utilize their assets at low cost, with high efficiency and quality.

In 1995, Zhang Ruimin transferred the 5,000 staff working at Haier Headquarters to the east of Qingdao High-tech Zone, and floated the concept of the 'second breakthrough'. Relying on this young, positive energy, Haier began acquiring dormant or failing enterprises to bring them back to life. It merged with eighteen different enterprises, representing a total inventory of ¥500 million in losses and ¥1.8 billion in assets, turning all of them around. Haier used mergers to develop and enhance competitiveness. Its acquisitions included the Shunde Washing Machine Factory in Guangdong, Fenghua Refrigerator Factory in Guizhou, and the Huangshan Television Factory in Hefei. Through this diversification and expansion of scope, Haier was able to find a broader space for development.

Haier's takeover targets all had common characteristics. The key point was that the technology, equipment and personnel quality were uniformly excellent in these companies, but they were mismanaged enterprises. Haier internally referred to this process as 'eating shocked fish'.

Zhang Ruimin says:

The goal of mergers is to use the minimum possible capital investment to rapidly expand the scope of the business. After the merger, corporate profitability should not depend on injecting large amounts of money into the new business, otherwise it would be better to build a new enterprise from scratch; instead, the profit should come from using our intangible assets, what we call brand operations, and by inputting our culture and management. Our approach was that the merged enterprise would copy the model used at Haier.

During the mergers, one of Haier's main tools was its culture. When Haier merged with Red Star Electrical Factory it produced washing machines, held net assets of only ¥100 million, and its losses amounted to ¥250 million. After the merger, Haier only sent three additional staff to Red Star and these were not from the Finance Department, but from the Corporate Cultural Centre. They continually talked with Red Star Factory staff about Haier's processes, and about their idea of applying Haier operational models to reactivate the factory. Apart from those three, the employees were all the same as before the merger, the equipment was still the original equipment, and the monthly loss in the month of the merger was ¥7 million. In the second month the losses were reduced, in the fifth month the company made a profit of more than ¥1 million. The difficulties with mergers are never technology and capital, but cultural applicability. When Chinese enterprises make expansion mergers, what is often missing is a clear business philosophy, or to put it another way, a clear corporate culture.

This merger became the subject of a Harvard Business School

case study by Lynn Paine and Robert Crawford. The authors noted that in the past, a company's performance was judged by looking at its books, whereas now, it depends more on the company's culture and the resulting cohesion, as this is the key to the company's ability to undergo sustainable development. The authors wanted to study successful companies because they wanted to know what good aspects of corporate culture affected the acquired company, and whether this was important for subsequent business development. The case studies noted that cultural cohesion has always been highly valued by Haier and attributed the company's success to this: 'The main factor in Haier's success was its corporate culture. Of course, technical and capital support is also very important, but without the right culture, Haier was able to take rigid and fixed assets and turn them into a source of value for every customer, employee, and investor and for society at large.'

Lynn Paine believes that the Haier culture includes some key values shared by the world's most ambitious companies:

1. Employees are given individual responsibility and initiative. Only where employees have a high degree of concern for the enterprise, and where there is a positive attitude to the role of employees at the company, is it possible to develop a vibrant corporate culture.

2. There is scope for continuous improvement and innovation. We should be able to sense a willingness to change and strong entrepreneurial energy in the corporate culture. Conservative enterprises with a moribund culture can only come to a standstill or slowly die.

3. The culture is focused on meeting customer needs. This does not just mean that it is necessary to meet customer requirements, but it also includes the intention to listen to customers, and capture their unexpressed inner thoughts, eliminating potential obstacles before the customers become dissatisfied.

A successful corporate culture is one in which all people truly feel they are valuable, and that the enterprise is socially responsible.

Moral principles and ethical engagement are indispensable parts of corporate culture.

Zhang Ruimin classes at Harvard

Paine says: 'These factors may sound vague and simple, but their operation is extremely difficult, especially when companies and employees are accustomed to working around plans, and taking the initiative is not encouraged.'

Zhang Ruimin, reflecting on why Haier was chosen as a Harvard case study commented, 'If your business is not very strong, then merging with a bad business could be crippling; if you are very strong, if your values and your management are very strong, you will be able to transform a weak business, no matter how poor it is.'

Shunde Haier Electric Group Limited was a successful low-cost expansion made in 1997 based on the application of this corporate culture. Again, after announcing the joint venture, Haier Washing Machine Division only sent three managers, but what they took with them were the management models and corporate culture developed over many years, along with strong research and development capacity. Six weeks later, the new company's first washing machine came off the assembly line, and this shocked fish had been brought back to life. Haier subsequently replicated this process many times.

Zhang Ruimin explains that the process of cultural integration was not always easy:

In one instance, Haier was merging with a television factory in Anhui. The merger took place in December 1997, and in that year the factory produced only 40,000 television sets; two years after the merger, they were producing 600,000 units. But in the beginning the merger was a strong collision. Enterprise workers went on strike and took to the streets because they could not accept Haier's management. Although they had very low wages, they were able to avoid working while on duty, so now, even though the salaries had been increased, they felt the management was too strict. Was Haier's management correct? We decided to postpone operations to discuss this issue for as long as it took. We had only discussed it with the employees for two days, when they recognized that if we did not succeed, they could not stand up in the market, and the enterprise would be untenable, employees would not receive any pay at all. Only when the company is successful can the employees do well. Through this discussion, many employees came to understand that it was not that Haier management was strict, but that market competition was harsh. In total we merged with eighteen companies, and the most difficult things to change were the original ideas held by the workers. However, if we could not change these concepts and ideas, it would be very difficult to run those companies successfully.

In the process of diversification, Haier explored the theory that the East shines then the West shines. This means that you must first become bigger, better and stronger in the industries you are most familiar with and only then can you enter into new industries. After reaching a certain size, jumps must be made to reach the forefront of the new industries.

In this way, Haier used a second seven-year period, built on the basis of the success of the brand strategy development, to create a new strategy of innovation and transfer. Through extending corporate culture and following the 'East shines then the West shines' model of development, the company was able to successfully implement diversification and expansion, so that the branded products developed into a full range of branded appliances, enhancing the company's overall strength.

Haier is the sea – flattening and informatization

Corporate culture is the carrier of people. Every organizational structure consists of people made of flesh and blood, so Zhang Ruimin has always firmly believed that the quality of people determines the quality of the product. In China's academic circles, there have always been two competing views pitching American management, with its emphasis on performance, against Japan's meticulous management methods. Zhang Ruimin's view on the debate is that he has always been an advocate of market results, so they should learn from both the Americans and the Japanese.

Using the benchmarks from GE and Toyota as goals, Zhang Ruimin placed his management focus on people, attempting to liberate their human capacity while at the same time employing systematic constraints that enabled the abilites of the workers to be leveraged.

In 1996, Haier implemented a Business Division system which has gained momentum year on year. The aim was to decentralize operations. This type of organization was first utilized by General Motors and DuPont, and combines centralized decision-making, with decentralized management. The organizational structure was pushed to its pinnacle by GE, but Haier was not just trying to imitate GE. Haier determined the level of decentralization according to its strategic needs.

The diversification strategy also let more people come to the fore. The Haier Business Division system was based on a cell division approach, allowing more promising enterprises to operate independently, thus avoiding the problem of rigid organization.

The organizational changes prioritized flattening and informatization. Flattening created a structure in which communication between levels was simplified. Informatization enabled both internal and external information to be learned in the quickest way possible. The overall strategy and deployment of resources was very clear, but specifically when applying it to the market, the competitiveness was formed by each of the business divisions.

In August 1999, in order to adapt to international developments, Haier's internal organizational structure saw a major adjustment, involving the establishment of logistics, commercial development (for Chinese as well as foreign business), and cash flow as well as an overseas business promotion division. This was the biggest restructuring in Haier's history. Logistics and commercial development were totally stripped out of their respective original divisions. Separating the logistics management in this way allowed the company to achieve the procurement of parts and raw materials from all over the world, so as to form a production line for the global distribution of materials, and create a global sales and distribution centre for the finished product, reducing costs, and improving competitiveness. Commercial development saw reduced costs and improved efficiency through the integration of resources; the cash flow division ensured the smooth transfer of funds as it was required.

The quality of staff comes from the quality of leadership

Haier's belief is that everyone has talent. The human resources process adopted the Chinese expression 'looking at horses is not as good a method of judging them as racing them' meaning that talent is not discerned by the leaders and managers, but becomes apparent through fair, just and open competition.

In 1996, Zhang Ruimin felt that Haier was always working within too small a scope, and that the Group should develop towards a wider range of products. He also felt that the lack of talent constituted a deadly bottleneck on the way forward. The question of how to enable good talent discovery was very difficult to solve. Inspired by the eagerness of the talented staff, Zhang Ruimin wrote an essay entitled 'Haier is the Sea'.

Zhang Ruimin boiled Haier's personnel philosophy down to four points:

One, giving a sense of fairness. Haier, through increased transparency, linked the way staff worked with their treatment, so as to give employees a sense of fairness. Second, giving a sense of accomplishment and respecting the achievements of the staff. Third, giving employees room for development. Leaders set the stage, allowing the staff to perform. Fourth, giving young cadres competitive opportunities.

In 1995, a mid-level manager complained about the 'poor quality of the staff'. Zhang Ruimin responded: 'The quality of staff is the quality of leadership.' He went on to say, 'The quality of your subordinates is not your responsibility, but if you cannot improve the quality of your subordinates, that is your responsibility.' Haier is good at finding weaknesses in the management, that is, the weakest link in the chain.

From the start, to address internal management level imbalances, Zhang Ruimin led Haier to select personnel from inside the company. The specific method to achieve this was the implementation of an up and down promotion system, so that workers were rotated and served in more than one position, allowing the talent of all the workers to grow. 'The deeper the dolphin dives, the higher it leaps,' goes the Chinese saying. This cycle ensured that the promoted workers were able to understand the most fundamental elements of the business. The deeper they sank the higher they could rise, and the greater their achievement.

At Haier, an excellent employee could progress from a team leader to a workshop director, all while working on the production system. But if he was to be promoted as a division leader, he would need marketing skills so he had to begin with the most basic work in marketing, and then move up step-by-step. Competent managers could go on to new posts; those that could not rise were removed.

This mechanism meant that when a worker applied to run higher-level departments Haier did not immediately let them take the post, instead asking them to undertake a period of basic training. Some workers may have already reached a very high position, but if they lacked the experience for a new job, they too would be sent to a more junior position. If they had experience in some aspects of the role, but had low overall ability, they were also sent for training. The pressure on the staff was high, but this helped to cultivate the overall ability of the workers.

As Haier's workers work their way up through the system, the result is that the current top managers were all once young employees who have grown along with the company, standing out among the competetion, and striving to become senior leaders. Supervision at Haier has always been rather strict. From the company to the various functional divisions, from each business unit to the factories, each worker has an evaluation form, divided into praise and criticism columns. Workers who receive praise are given additional points (salary) and those who receive criticism have their points reduced (fines). After years of operation, the praise and criticism system now forms part of Haier's infrastructure. It is common for senior leaders to be criticized. What they work hardest to avoid is being criticized in the in-house publication *Haier People*.

Zhang Ruimin – upwardly (and downwardly) mobile, transparent and fair

Haier's internal structure changes constantly, but there is little changeover in personnel. This may be because of the culture of Haier; when we had just started business, every month there was a criticism and praise session targeted at the company's workers. The first effect was psychological; they got used to it. They got used to the ups and downs, and eventually they felt like they were normal and nothing remarkable. Many SOEs came to us to see how we operated, and learned this one thing from us. It cannot be done in one or two days, but requires long-term effort.

Second, we had strong requirements from the very beginning. Everything had to be transparent, no cliques were allowed to form, and no one was permitted to work with small teams of friends at the expense of the wider company.

I think that fairness is very important. I was from a poor background, had served as a worker, and I worked at the grassroots level for many years. As someone who was subject to management from higher-ups, at that time, the thing I longed for most was simple: fairness. If we had a fair environment, I would work very hard, and I believe everyone else would do the same thing. When I served as a manager, I tried to build and promote a fair corporate culture, so within Haier we attempted to create transparent relationships.

At one point in a two-year period 2,000 students joined the company. This is a huge number of new recruits. Each student had his or her own career development plan. Whatever level they wanted to reach, I would design a road for them, so that if they worked hard, they could rise to the position they wanted to reach. Of course, this was linked to performance. When you go upwards, this is mainly due to your competitiveness. Every month we held a meeting for high-level managers, and every month, we evaluated the results of their monthly innovations.

4

Haier's internationalization (1998–2005)

The Internet age – bubbles everywhere

In 1998, two Stanford students Larry Page and Sergey Brin registered a company named Google.

In January 2000, Li Yanhong, and Xu Yong created Baidu in Zhongguancun, Beijing, committed to providing simple and reliable access to information. They developed Baidu to become the world's largest Chinese search engine, and beat Google in the Chinese market.

This was a time of mania on the stock market which led to the Internet bubble, the investment crisis that occurred between 1995 and 2001 affecting the information technology and Internet industry. In the European, American and Asian stock markets, Internet and information technology-related companies saw their stock prices rising rapidly, but on 10 March 2000, the Nasdaq index hit a high of 5408.60. The combination of soaring stock prices and buyer speculation, as well as extensive use of venture capital, created a breeding ground for these companies to abandon the traditional business model. A standard dot-com business model depends on continuous network effects, wherein long-term operation losses were incurred to gain market share. The companies expected to build enough brand awareness to harvest for profits through services at a later stage. Quick growth was the favoured strategy. These businesses broke with the traditional model which focused more on the bottom line.

Historically, the economic growth of the Internet can be viewed as similar to that of other technologies – including the railways of the 1840s, the automobiles and radios of the 1920s, the transistors of the 1950s, and the time-sharing computers of the 1960s, as well as the home computers and biotechnology of the 1980s.

The dot-com model was inherently flawed: a large number of companies in the same field had the same business plan which was to monopolize the network effect. Obviously, even if the plan was good, there could only be one winner for each area, so most companies with the same business plans would fail. In fact, many sectors did not even have the ability to support a single large business. Finally, this led to the Nasdaq index falling to 1172.06 points in September 2002, a loss of 77 per cent of total market capitalization. Many companies went bankrupt.

Social networks

After the dot-com bubble burst the sector returned to a state of rational development. People's enthusiasm for the Internet skyrocketed as its involvement in our lives deepened, especially with the advent of Internet-based social interaction.

In 2004, just a few months after Google was listed, Harvard's Mark Zuckerberg created a website open only to Harvard students that would later develop into Facebook, the international social-networking site. Facebook quickly took over the social networking space previously occupied by MySpace.

E-commerce

In July 1994, Jeff Bezos founded Amazon. The business started as an online bookstore, and shortly afterwards underwent diversification. On 15 May 1997, Amazon was listed on the Nasdaq. Its first business plan was very different to that of its competitors: it did not anticipate achieving a large profit within four to five years, in fact, quite the contrary. Its slow growth caused a lot of shareholder complaints, as the investors believed that they were not making a fast enough return on their investments. They felt that the company would not even be able to survive among the competition. However, Amazon survived the dot-com bubble and ultimately became the Internet's retail giant. In the fourth quarter of 2001, Amazon made its first profits. Bezos' non-traditional business model was a success.

In December 1998, Ma Yun and seventeen other founders launched China's first Internet trading market in Hangzhou, Alibaba Online. In 1999, Wang Juntao entered the field of e-commerce with 8848 and Shao Yibo founded the first Chinese C2C e-commerce platform, eachnet.com. Joyo and Dangdang were set up in 2000. In the same year, China Merchants Bank took the lead in starting up the Yiwangtong online banking service, becoming the first commercial bank to carry out online personal banking. In 2000, the number of Internet users in China was quite small, only about 10 million, but the Internet lifestyle no longer remained in the e-mail and news browsing domains. In this immature market, B2C e-commerce sites such as 8848 were regarded as the shining bright spots of a new world, but ultimately failed.

In May 2003, SARS broke out, and made online shopping feel like the safer option. The number of members of B2B and B2C e-commerce sites increased rapidly. What is more, they made some profit, and the situation in C2C also improved. In that same month, Alibaba Group invested ¥100 million to set up Taobao, entering the field of C2C. In October 2003, it launched Alipay, then Amazon reached an agreement to acquire Joyo for $75 million, and changed its Chinese name to Amazon Joyo. Elsewhere, the Jingdong multimedia network (later renamed JD.com) and Tencent Paipai were established in 2004 and 2005.

Over the next few years a domestic C2C market structure was gradually formed in China, and online shopping became more and more popular. At the same time, e-business infrastructure continued to mature as logistics, payment and integrity bottlenecks were basically resolved. In the B2B, B2C, and C2C fields many online retailers saw rapid growth, accumulating a large number of e-commerce operations and acquiring financial management experience. Countless traditional enterprises and funds began to enter, so e-commerce quickly became a domain outside the control of mere Internet companies.

Dancing with wolves – privatization

In September 1999, the Fourth Plenary Session of the Fifteenth CPC saw a motion to raise a Decision on Some Major Issues of SOE Reform and Development, strategically adjusting the state's economic layout, saying that China should 'allow the opening and closing of businesses, allowing them to behave as they wish'. One year later, Professor Wang Jue from the Central Party School of the Communist Party of China issued the report 'Workers shared ownership system and socialist market economics – Thoughts on Strategic Integration of Socialism and Market Economics'. For the first time, this raised the notion of privatization in the public realm. Although the saying, 'the state retreats, the private sector advances' was not accurate in describing the state-owned economic restructuring and SOE property reform, his words were reported widely in the Chinese media and spread like wildfire.

In 2002, at the Sixteenth Communist Party Congress, proposals were made for improving the socialist market economic system, bringing the rounds of SOE reform to a new peak. In spring 2003, the state-owned Assets Supervision and Administration Commission was born. This is considered a key stage in the separation of the state from enterprises on the one hand, and governments from funding on the other, so that SOEs could move towards the market, forming independent competitive organizations.

Although it was a major strategic adjustment to SOE, privatization did not include reform to the statewide legal system. A trial and error approach was adopted in each location, so that the right path could be followed according to the different contexts. Management MBOs, roundabout MBOs, ESOPs, bankruptcy restructurings, to name just a few, were mobilized and given legal regulatory powers, forming the most significant features of this round of privatization.

After 2004, there was a period of controversy about the direction of the reform of SOEs. Hong Kong-based finance professor Lang Xianping was a prominent, and vocal, critic of the direction the changes were moving in. He criticized the 'loss of state assets and SOE reform model'. In a sense, he started an accountability movement for the state asset privatization process concluding that while he was not opposed to the reform of SOEs, he was opposed to some of the methods for selling them. Haier was only peripherally involved in this debate when it was mistakenly assumed to be an SOE; in fact Haier is a collectively owned enterprise, and COEs have always had a very different enterprise structure and accountability system.

The legacy of this dispute still exists in the question of how to avoid the loss of state assets during reforms. What is more, the fears of private enterprises about merging with or purchasing state-owned assets have not yet been resolved.

In 2007, there was an adjustment to public–private property relations and the definition, recognition and protection of property rights were established in property law. This law offered further legal protection and institutionalization of property rights, and moved the thinking away from *reform* of property rights to the *protection* of private property rights.

China's WTO accession

For China, 10 November 2001 was a historic day. That afternoon, the WTO held their Fourth Ministerial Conference in Doha, Qatar, with all participating countries reaching a consensus approving China's accession to the WTO. China's MOFTEC Minister Shi Guangsheng signed the protocol on behalf of the Chinese government. On 11 December, China became the 143rd member of the WTO. WTO Director General Mike Moore told reporters of the Xinhua News Agency: 'China's WTO accession is the proudest moment of my life.' This marked China's full return to the world economic stage.

Just before and after China's accession to the WTO, predicting the future direction of China's economic circle became a popular pastime. The Ministry of International Trade and Industry was the first to mention in a white paper that China had become the 'world's factory'. For colour TVs, washing machines, refrigerators, air conditioners, microwave ovens, motorcycles and other products, 'Made in China' products ranked first among the world's market share. Many economists further believed that China would be like Japan in the 1980s, and was just beginning a journey to conquer the world.

Haier 'Made in China'

For most of the 1990s, Haier was actively preparing for one thing – shipping goods across oceans.

In 1994, China had not yet rejoined GATT and foreign appliances were making inroads into the Chinese market. Zhang Ruimin declared that Haier was ready to challenge the international brands: 'Tougher market challenges have emerged and dealing with this competition is like dancing with wolves. The result will be either victory over the wolves, or being eaten by the wolves.'

In February 1996, Zhang Ruimin wrote 'Not a New Year Message' for *Haier People* magazine. In it he discussed the crisis presented by foreign brands manufacturing in China: 'the combination of international brands and low-costs mean terrifying competitiveness'. Internationalization gradually became the first item on the company's agenda.

Haier's unique international strategy was 'do the hard things first, then do the easy things'. This meant first opening the markets of developed countries, then entering them. The company decided to use the three thirds business structure, that is, domestic production and domestic sales acounts for one third; domestic production with foreign sales accounts for one third; and foreign production with foreign sales accounts for one third. The third here does not refer to the sales volumes, but the three different business forms.

In Haier's three thirds, the first third was to be realized by local Haier offices, such as Hefei Haier and Guizhou Haier; the second third by Qingdao Haier through product exports; and the third by American Haier and European Haier through design, production and sales.

According to the strategic plan of 'doing the hard things first, then the easy things', in 1999, Haier invested $30 million to establish a 445,000 square metre production centre in South Carolina in the United States with a view to first entering the highly competitive US market, so that access to other countries would be relatively easy. Haier's idea was to 'find masters to play chess'. But this process presented obvious difficulties, as the wages of workers in South Carolina were nineteen times that of wages in China, and the pure cost competitive advantage was far less noticeable.

Through the establishment of the factory in South Carolina, Haier clarified a going out, coming in, and then going up 'three-step' strategy. The 'three-step' strategy was simply to first, achieve internationalization through the integration of global resources, and export products overseas; second, achieve the localization of the brand on the international market, so as to become a locally recognized product, entering the local chain, with local design, and providing a service to local customers; and third, relying on this localization, to become a local brand. In the United States for example, meeting the needs of local consumers in the United States could not be done without the South Carolina plant.

Haier relied on columns rather than horizontals for market development. This involved making a breakthrough in the United States using small refrigerators, then moving to washing machines, air conditioning, etc., before finally progressing into the entire appliance industry. Once the US plant was running with no problems, a plant in Pakistan was also successfully constructed. A single breakthrough would open up wider spaces.

In June 2001, Haier invested $5 million to acquire the factory of the Italian refrigerator manufacturer Mainigaidi. This was considered by many to be an unwise decision, but Haier now sells high-end products in Germany produced in the Italian factory. Through this process of cross-border mergers and acquisitions, Haier created a white goods production base in Europe.

Chinese enterprises often struggle to understand the international market, which makes it difficult for them to determine the correct strategy for development. Haier realized that this was an issue and took steps to minimize the market risks when expanding internationally. Haier decided on a 'market before factory' principle. Being competitive was the prerequisite for establishing an overseas factory. The break-even point for building a local refrigerator plant in the United States was an annual output of around 300,000 units. Haier's annual refrigerator exports to the United States reached more than half a million units before the company decided to invest in establishing its own factory.

Between 1998 and 2005, Haier established 18 overseas factories, 17 marketing companies, and 9 R&D centres. The integration of R&D with the overseas manufacturing and overseas marketing achieved the goal of creating the best of all worlds.

Zhang Ruimin – Creating own brand

At that time, our colleagues in the industry felt it was better to live on soup in China than go overseas to survive on bones, so they went on with licensing agreements, rather than building a brand. We believed that with China joining the WTO, among other factors, the wolf was at our door, and if we wanted to dance with the wolf we would have to become a wolf ourselves. I met an overseas student in Germany in 2012, who said that a German business school teacher told them that the reason Haier was able to succeed was because when large multinational companies entered China, only Haier had aspired to becoming a 'Super Wolf'. At that time, many Chinese enterprises felt that they could not compete with the multinational enterprises, so they let them dominate the cities, while moving to the countryside. However, the international companies have a winner takes all strategy – they did not just want the cities, they also wanted the rural areas.

When I went to Germany, the price of our products five years before had been just a fraction of the price of European local brands. People were selling products for more than €1,300, whereas we were not even able to sell ours at €300. But then we were very confident, because although our products were put in the corner, not being noticed, we were the only Chinese brand available. Now when I go to Europe, I see that not only are our products being sold for more than €1,300, but they are more expensive than some brand-name products sold in Europe. This is because we unswervingly created our own brand from the outset. In the early days, because Haier products were getting good customer feedback, we were offered a deal to supply Haier refrigerators to be sold under an American brand name. However, we told the agent this was impossible as we were not willing to jeopardize our brand globally.

Process re-engineering – market chains

The years from 1998 to 2005 were a seven-year international strategy phase. Haier focused on building a brand rather than just selling overseas. By sailing across the sea, it began to turn from a small fish in a small pond to a big fish in the sea.

However, this evolutionary process was painful. Zhang Ruimin discovered that getting the opportunity to compete with international giants would require restructuring business processes. As a result, from 1998 onwards, Haier began a comprehensive process of re-engineering. From a global perspective this re-engineering was unprecedented for a large enterprise, it was market-oriented, with the goal of allowing the company to respond quickly to the needs of users, using a flat organizational structure.

The first stage of the re-engineering was Zhang Ruimin's market chain theory. As Haier diversified in the 1990s expansion, Zhang Ruimin discovered that Haier was still lacking the requirements for future development. In accordance with the principles of the customer economy, the first concern for any business is customer satisfaction, the second is speed, and the third is the error rate. Although Haier had already moved into the outside world, the company found it was difficult to achieve excellence in these three factors while maintaining the traditional Chinese organizational structure. The traditional structure follows a pyramid design, so that the enterprise and the market form two separate pyramids, meaning that numerous gaps exist between the enterprise level and market-side employees. This means that market information is not correctly and quickly passed forward, resulting in increased inventory and non-performing assets. More importantly, user needs are not fully satisfied within this system.

The market chain Zhang Ruimin proposed was designed to resolve these issues by answering the question of how the enterprise can truly perceive the market. Changes were made so that the staff were responsible to the market rather than to their superiors, with everyone facing the market, while at the same time being a market themselves. The SST mechanism was introduced, an acronym for the Chinese terms meaning 'claim compensation, claim payment and stop'. Claiming compensation means providing goods and services to clients through the market chain, thereby obtaining compensation from the market. Claiming payment applies between departments in the market chain, where the upstream and downstream departments form a mutual relationship. If either party cannot deliver on their promises, the downstream department may claim for a payment. The stop aspect refers to acting as a stop valve so that if neither claims nor compensation can be made, a third party will stop the process.

The internal market chain includes the information / development / manufacturing / pre-sales / sales / after-sales / information closed loop. The user requirements determine the product's potential competitiveness, the direction of development towards solving the user's problems and the quality standard.

Zhang Ruimin said of these changes:

Logistics use time to remove space; commercial flows use space to eliminate time. We broke with all previous management functions, creating a process with variable functions. With the new process, all commercial flows were built around orders … In the new economy, each employee was given personalized room for innovation, so as to meet the needs of individual consumers.

If the proposed market chains were designed to bring about better internationalization, so that the enterprises could stand on the same platform as the international brands, then the market chain implementation was based around moving the enterprise towards information technology. Top grade information technology is the basis for ensuring smooth operations. Since then, Haier has set up a model in which information technology is used to provide services to users.

Zhang Ruimin – Bringing the external market inside

I wanted to ensure that a worker's pay would not be determined by their boss, but that the market should have the final say. Who is your market? It is the next step in your workflow. For example, for buyers of raw materials, the user is the market, so if the raw materials are not good, they will claim from him. Whereas the producers' market are the testers. If problems occur during testing, this means the inspector can claim compensation from the producer on behalf of the users. After entering the market, as the salesperson sells the products, the after-sales service staff are the market of the sales staff.

In the past there was no internal market, so only after entering the real external market, could people claim payment from you if any problems arose. Now this was changed, the external market was moved inside, so we call this the internal market chain. The implementation of this market chain was very, very difficult, as we needed to be very thin. At that time, I said to my colleagues, if we do this, we will not need to be afraid of anyone.

What kind of concept is this? It is that everyone has a market, and each person is also a market themselves. No longer is it the case that when you work better, we will give you more money, when you work more you get more money. The market does not give you money for working more. Everyone has performance indicators, and if there are no indicators applicable to your work, then you are laid off, as you are no longer needed.

Taking designers as an example, their money comes from the market, so they can take ¥10,000 if they design a good product. They have laboratory personnel working underneath them; last month those lab staff could take ¥2,000. But now? There is no money. The money is with the designer, so the lab personnel would ask the designer what work needs to be done. For example, three experiments may be required, with a fee paid for each experiment. If your work for a month totals less than ¥1,500, this means you have not produced value. So lab personnel are desperate to find a living. In the past, at factories, this position was the most comfortable. Then there are the artists within a company. In the past they could say, if you give me a picture to draw, I will draw it, but if you do not give it to me, I can be idle.

There must be full labour management. It was sometimes difficult to get acceptance from the junior levels. But I think that if you do a good job, even if efficiency is not greatly improved, at least psychological problems are solved for some people. Now, there are over 20,000 employees, and I could not possibly look after them myself. Staff will always make comparisons: he didn't do much work today, he took two hours for relaxation. However, asking managers to see clearly who did more and who did less work, and who has earned their wages is impossible, and if this power is transmitted downwards, leaders at all levels would have privileges, so if you are good to me I will give you an advantage of some kind, if not I can kick you out of the company. There would be no way to avoid this. Therefore, the benefits or penalties you gain should be determined by your market rather than by your supervisor.

Information revolution

In April 2000, Zhang Ruimin published 'My views on the "New Economy"' in the *Haier People* magazine, giving a summary of his experience of participating in the Davos Forum that year. In the article, he proposed that Haier's road through the new economy should be what he called *enterprise informatization*:

> *The Internet means you cannot be complacent, it reduces the distances to zero, the traditional continuity is broken and the traditional structures have vanished. Lacking new ideas is effectively giving up. Next are the innovations in operational*

*models, including institutional and organizational struc-
tures, and so on. Our organization should become an ordered
non-equilibrium structure, and internal processes should be
adapted to the changing external market. Another round of
new technology innovation is needed, using the advantages
of the Internet to utilize global scientific and technological
resources, creating new demand through innovation and
technology and thus creating new markets. Not utilizing the
Internet means death.*

Zhang Ruimin's passion was born of a dawning realization about
what companies like Wal-Mart and Dell were capable of. Wal-
Mart has an accurate grasp of every store, every consumer and
every product, and Dell's 20-second ordering made Zhang Ruimin sigh, and conclude: 'Just staying in the market to compete,
and competing with products will never be enough.'

China had never had its own management system. Zhang Ruimin believed that effective use of information technology was the
only way to turn the latecomer disadvantage into an advantage.
This information revolution covered Haier's two strategic phases:
its internationalization strategy and its brand globalization strategy. Facing global competition without informatization would
have made Haier unmanageable though, as even then, Chinese
enterprises were still finding inventory and accounts receivable to
be great headaches.

Another reason that Zhang Ruimin implemented the information revolution for Haier was to turn people into the main car-
riers of innovation, 'to provide each employee with the maximum
space for results, creating the shortest information chain by flattening the shared information and organization structure using
the Internet. This would allow self-management, personal challenges, and reflection of our own values and the results of our
own innovation, forming a strong force for team cohesion.'

Tracking everyone using information technology so as to
achieve self-quantification was the first step in the liberation of
the innate abilities of all who worked at the company.

Everyone becomes a Strategic Business Unit (SBU)

In 2003, Zhang Ruimin proposed the idea of converting Haier's 30,000 employees into 30,000 self-managed SBUs. The goal of this was that everyone would become an innovative resource.

The four elements of the SBU are the four goals of the enterprise, now transferred to each person:

- **Market targets:** Competitiveness through rapidly reflecting the market and creating user resources.

- **Market orders:** Orders to create valuable innovation, bringing about market targets.

- **Market effect:** Implementing orders to create user satisfaction data, and displaying this on the enterprise information systems.

- **Market returns:** Income reflected from the market value you have created, and the scope to further increase your ability to meet market needs.

SBU objectives for enterprises, employees and users are all different. The idea for staff is to become the 'bodies of innovation', creating value for users, and bringing about their own value. This is a kind of self-management process; if everyone becomes an SBU they form the backbone of the competitiveness of the enterprise. This is something competitors cannot imitate or copy. For the users, this means helping them develop corporate and brand loyalty in the Internet age. If each employee is innovating, no matter how the user's needs change, Haier can always seize the opportunities presented.

After the re-engineering process at Haier, marketing staff were renamed 'client managers'. At the same time, their responsibilities were completely changed, so that they no longer just had to get orders for the products, but instead had to complete four tasks: help improve customer sales, help improve gross profit margins, help improve cash flow rates, and help to fully resolve customer problems. After adopting this system, a large number of independent innovative SBUs appeared in Haier's research, marketing, manufacturing, and service sectors, innovating to meet the needs of users, in order to gain market recognition and praise.

The reason Haier made an effort to create such a mechanism was that Zhang Ruimin believed that in the Information Age enterprises should rely on personalization. Only by moving from mass production to mass customization, and by quickly meeting the needs of different users can enterprises win. So the question is: how does Haier achieve mass customization? How does it meet the individual needs of users?

Information technology is characterized by rapid changes, therefore companies should also have adaptive decision-making abilities. Those kinds of decisions must be based on employee initiatives. Only through this may companies do the right things as well as doing things right. To achieve the goal of alignment with market requirements, everyone had to become a resource.

They all became independent, self-financing enterprises. Generally, the teams were given three key tables – balance sheet, income statement, and cash flow statement. When Haier initiated human resources reform, an SBU operations form was used to show the staff the content of these three key tables. At the same time, on the basis of an ERP system based on SAP, the personal income and results of each individual were connected.

Zhang Ruimin – everyone directly faces the market

We now use computers to try to match market data with each employee, so that we can meet customer needs in the fastest way. So the question was how to move this complex internal data to every individual, so that everyone could have an operations table showing their goals and achievements. The three tables (balance sheet, income statement, and cash flow statement) became part of everyone's income statements. But the most important point about this is that Haier staff no longer have a fixed salary, instead, the greater the benefits you create for the enterprise, the greater the salary you get. In addition, the enterprise's assets are broken down to the level of individual employees. Let's say you join our business, the desk, computer and so on are not free to use. The designer's wages are cancelled, that is to say that the designer can not get money simply by designing products, but only after the designed products reach the market, the income will be determined depending on the margins and sales. Everyone is fully connected to the market. When designing, the designer must fully understand the market, and understand what the users actually require, otherwise they would not be able to design the products that people want, so they could not get any benefits.

In the Internet era, the market changes very quickly, and the space for business to grow is increasing, expanding to cover the entire planet. However, the distance from the enterprise to the user requirements is getting shorter, shortening to zero. Whoever meets the needs of users on the Internet in the quickest way will be the winner. Everyone must directly face the market, rather than working to the requirements of their superiors. We hoped to explore a new model, so that everyone could continue to innovate, creating valuable orders, and thereby creating value for the product users. By creating value for the users, the value of the employees can be realized, and 'big company disease' can be prevented. I hoped that however large we became, we would be able to quickly meet market requirements, and always be full of vitality!

Visual management

Without the support of information systems, no employee can get the data required for decision-making, and they are less likely to produce a good SBU operations table. The Haier revolution was built on the platform of information systems.

Since 2002, Haier has insisted on the use of barcodes, including the 'item code' and 'man code'. The item code is the bar code affixed to each product. The man code is the number Haier gives for each workstation. The reason why the number is assigned to stations rather than people is because sometimes people move around. Thus, the station code is equivalent to a person's barcode. Haier puts the man code and item code on the documents for all operations, and no matter how complex the business is, no matter how fast the process runs, it can be easily managed. All these actions rely on information technology.

Zhang Ruimin believes that: 'It is a mistake to do daily management by hand in the information age. When purchasing from Wal-Mart, everything is displayed on a computer, so headquarters can see sales information at a glance. My question was why couldn't we do that?'

What Zhang Ruimin wanted was to make the business processes and any enterprise information clear to everyone. Making the enterprise information crystal clear is not only a good way to cope with the needs of regulatory agencies and capital markets, but is also a good way for the CEO to achieve business process control, thereby enhancing the competitiveness of the enterprise.

Individual goals together

In September 2005, Haier held the 2005 Global Managers' Meeting, at which Zhang Ruimin proposed the 'individual goals together' global competition Haier model. This new thinking was presented as the source of future global competitiveness for Haier.

Within the phrase, 'individuals' refers to every employee, and is also the subject of each person's autonomous innovation.

'Goals' refers to competitive market goals. Zhang Ruimin explains that 'individual goals together' means that everyone has their own goals, and is responsible for them and that there is some- one responsible for each goal. The goals are the market so that every individual is linked to the market and the quality of the staff and the quantity of orders are proportional. That is, the higher the quality of the people, the higher the quantity of orders, the higher the value created by the orders. What is more, in this way, inventories and receivables are not produced. The order creates the value in the market, bringing about the value of the people. Therefore, revenue and goals should be linked for everyone. 'Indi- vidual goals together' means that the market is bound to each per- son and everyone operates directly on the market.

The logic is that companies cannot continue to work towards fixed targets – thinking they have time to slowly take aim, and slowly research objectives. This era no longer exists. While you are trying to clarify the market research opportunities, the opportu- nities will have already evaporated. Haier requires each employee to directly face the market, so every person's orders are related to their market and they can capture that market. This means the company has a uniform speed and accuracy that enables it to get the numbers needed to survive.

Haier puts the individual goals together into three steps: the first is the design order, the second is the release of Haier prod- ucts, and the third is the recovery of the price. This closed-loop process links the start to the finish.

The designer goals are not about designing a particular kind of product and asking how many people want it but, according to market demand, creating the appropriate products for the known market. The design order is essentially a design market. The per- son in charge of Haier's American plant proposed that when prod- ucts were being designed, the design order and the price/benefit/ amount be taken into account. The 'price' means, for example, the product may sell for $2,000, and have good market return, 'ben- efit' means how many units will cover the cost to the American factory, and 'amount' refers to how many units must be sold.

Because products are designed based on needs which have been clearly determined, they can be sent directly to the market, directly to the user, the money for the goods can be recovered immediately, and this forms a virtuous circle. Direct sales are very important to Haier because it saves on costs associated with storing products which would otherwise reduce returns on sales.

The whole process requires an SBU to implement the individual goals together system and to control the entire process. This demands a lot of promotion of sub-processes and there are many steps to complete.

Finally, a market-oriented corporate culture can be formed by installing a direct sales team in which the designers, marketers, manufacturers, sales staff and customers, jointly develop products to meet the market's next requirements. If you can form such a cultural atmosphere, individual goals together can make an enterprise highly competitive.

If everyone at Haier is involved in innovation, and each person's potential is immeasurable, then the sum of these will certainly be greater than that of any other company. The core spirit of individual goals together is the high degree of integration of people with the market. Its purpose is to fully stimulate the potential of each employee so that each person's potential to achieve business goals is released, while the business goals are aligned with everyone's potential. With such a high degree of integration, Haier would eliminate the three remaining obstacles which cause tremendous headaches for every company: invalid orders, inventories, and accounts receivable.

Fully results-based

By unifying the market chain with people, Zhang Ruimin created a kind of 'shock' environment at Haier. For employees, this means a highly competitive Darwinian corporate culture. The Haier employee evaluation system is personal (team work is not evaluated), immediate (instant rewards and punishments after the work is completed) and quantitative (based on the amount of work created and the level of losses incurred, with little consideration of personal effort, attitude, motivation or other factors), and open (evaluation rules and the results are open to all, so workers can calculate their wages, with the management's subjective evaluation covering just a few components). It is results-oriented, focusing on financial motivation via 'negative incentives' (this is the Haier term tantamount to punishment with the aim that employees stop making the same mistakes, rather than simply paying the price for them), wages are calculated according to degree of achievement/performance on the market. Age, gender, education, length of service and so on are not reward factors. During personnel promotions and transfers, there is competition for position and dynamic adjustment, with a strong focus on market mechanisms. The results rarely stem from the judgment of superiors or the personnel department, rather the '10/10 principle' is used: each year, the top performing 10 per cent are elevated as role-models and the worst performing 10 per cent are dismissed. If you are in the last 10 per cent in your first year, the company sends you for training, if you are still in the last 10 per cent in the second year, you have to go for training but you pay for it yourself. In your third year, if you are still in the last 10 per cent, you must leave.

Haier does not manage managers on the basis of job responsibilities, but around the market, implementing the 'three focuses doctrine'. That is: completely focusing on orders in the market, completely focusing on results in work distribution, and completely focusing on first place in results. These requirements change the distribution relationships, so that the value of each employee is shown in the creation of value for users, and is not dependent on his or her position. During process re-engineering, everyone was to become a contact point, so managers first had to transform themselves into contact points. The thing to highlight in relation to this is that within the Haier Group, the vice presidents are not in charge of routine management, but they are also personally working to hit targets for respective business divisions. There are vice presidents for mobile phones, home furnishings, computers and television divisions, who are evaluated in the same way as the directors of other divisions. The market's reach covers virtually all the staff at Haier.

This is an experiment in 'zero middle layer'. It is not that managers are not wanted at Haier, but there is no need for layer upon layer of management, each person should be allowed to directly face the market. Previously, senior staff could command subordinates, but now everyone is subordinate to the customers. For example, in the 'claim compensation, claim payment and stop' system, if problems occur due to the service of superiors being poor, subordinates can confidently claim against them. Zhang Ruimin hoped that in this way Haier would form a win-win business philosophy where leaders help employees succeed, and employees help customers succeed. As he says, 'we are only successful when everyone succeeds.'

Kobe University professor Hideki Yoshihara compared Haier's management with that of Japan and the United States. His final conclusion was that Haier's market management mechanisms are more thorough than either. Haier's management can be regarded as almost the exact opposite of Japanese management: the Japanese emphasize teamwork and collective performance; employee evaluation not only looks at results but also personal effort and attitude; evaluation rules, procedures, and results are not disclosed; during the promotion of personnel, the personnel department's evaluation has a critical influence, internal personnel changes brought about by open competition are limited; loyalty and discipline occupy a certain position in the evaluation system; the seniority-wage system is implemented, there is a focus on long-term evaluation, and the sacking of managers is extremely rare. Because Japanese-style management is based more on psychological and sociological considerations, introducing performance-related pay systems in Japanese companies is very easily frustrated.

In recent years, as Japanese electronics companies entered the red, they became very concerned about their salary systems. In 2003, at the first domestic enterprise management seminar in

Japan, Nissan, Toyota and Sony each made corporate statements, talking about how the wage-seniority system created large problems for enterprise development. They wanted to break with the system, and they hoped to borrow the thinking of Haier.

Hideki Yoshihara says that American management mechanisms for the production side of the enterprise are not focused on the market. Workers get a fixed salary, jobs cannot be arbitrarily changed, and there is a 'first in last out' culture. New recruits begin with short contracts and as people work longer the wages and security increase; middle managers and professional and technical personnel are managed with only limited market mechanisms; a CEO may make millions of dollars of salary, but they must reach their business goals, or risk being dismissed immediately. Yoshihara concludes that in general, China's management style has more in common with the American than the Japanese system but Haier has gone even further than American corporations.

Zhang Ruimin used to take Japanese and American managers as his role models, but now feels that Haier's market chain model is doing a good job, and foreign companies could learn from Haier. Wharton management professor Marshall Meyer noted: 'Everything is absolutely transparent to employees, from product development to production to sales, everyone knows what is happening along the whole chain. This is something which has been inculcated at all levels within Haier.' He went on: 'Every employee has in mind a picture of the entire organization, and understands how each part is linked. If you ask a person where orders come from, he'll tell you who the customer is. If the sales staff are not able to recover the purchase price, they will not earn any wages.'

5

Haier's globalization (2005–2012)

Birth of the iPhone and mobile culture

On 9 January 2007, human society entered the 'i' era. On this day the iPhone was presented to the world by Steve Jobs at the Moscone Center in San Francisco. The phone had a 3.5-inch screen, the body had no physical keyboard, and users only required a home button and sliding gestures to complete all necessary functions. Jobs said: 'We have reinvented the phone.'

The iPhone adhered to the minimalist modern industrial aesthetic ideas that Apple had always pursued; it was precise, delicate, and fine. However, this time Apple had created more than just a well-made mobile phone with a revolutionary user interface, it also introduced the new mobile computing paradigm. When the App Store launched, one application after the next formed a self-sufficient world, which made it possible to exclusively exist in mobile devices. The phone started to be able to support a variety of human needs. This opened up areas that web giants such as Google could not reach, a new platform which HTML could not rule.

On 27 January 2010, having subverted the mobile phone industry, Jobs created a new market: tablet computers. Dubbed the iPad, the new product sat between mobile phones and laptops, and like the iPhone, had a minimalist design, with the same operating system, and the same software platform. It offered a better reading and viewing experience than the iPhone.

On 6 October 2011, Steve Jobs died of pancreatic cancer, at the age of 56.

Even though Silicon Valley is filled with superstars of technology, Jobs was its brightest star. How far did his greatness reach? In a nutshell: he started the computing revolution, and then he subverted it.

In the 1990s, Silicon Valley had almost no relationship to mobile technology. Now, Silicon Valley has become the epicentre of this revolutionary movement. All of these things happened only because Apple developed the iPhone. The iPhone and iPad together marked the end of the PC era, putting human beings into the mobile era.

Steve Jobs not only created the world's most innovative and valuable technology company, he also reshaped Silicon Valley; he invented a series of cool, shiny consumer electronics products, and changed the way people associate with their technology, leading them towards a global digital culture.

The Twitter era

In 2006, Jack Dorsey posted a message, 'Just setting up my twttr'. Subsequently, this application which allowed users to express their feelings in 140 characters took the world into a social networking frenzy. At the birth of the company in 2006, there were only 50 users; Twitter now has more than 300 million active users worldwide.

During those years of growth, Twitter users have published more than 400 million tweets. People use Twitter to update their own information, share news, and entertain fans. Twitter completely changed people's behaviour and heralded the 'Sharing Era'.

On 14 August 2009, Sina began closed beta testing of a sharing tool called Weibo. Most people think of this as the Chinese version of Twitter. As celebrities started to adopt the new platform, the number of registered users quickly exceeded 100 million. In December 2012, the number of users on Weibo broke the 500 million mark. The scenes you will see when you look around in China, as a result of Weibo, whether on the subway, or on the street, and especially at gatherings, will generally be people looking downwards at small screens, or stopping to take pictures to share. Sharing has almost become synonymous with the word Weibo.

In 2011 Tencent launched a new piece of voice communications software, WeChat, which allows users to quickly send text, photos and chat, once again changing the way people exchange and share information. WeChat is seen by many as showing the way to social media's future; for its users it acts as a hub for all internet activity, and as a platform for finding other services. The slogan on the official WeChat website is 'WeChat is a way of life'.

At the end of March 2012, the number of WeChat users broke through the 100 million mark, only 433 days after launch. WeChat made Weibo nervous, made the telecom operators nervous, and even made the two Internet giants Baidu and Alibaba nervous. The development of WeChat was like finding a gold mine.

The financial crisis and the revival of the manufacturing sector

On 15 September 2008, the 158-year-old bank Lehman Brothers filed for bankruptcy protection. This bankruptcy showed that the US subprime crisis was bringing the 'too big to fail' capitalist system down. The subprime crisis slowly began to transform into a global financial crisis.

The crisis originally referred to the subprime crisis in the United States, specifically relating to the storm caused by a succession of bankrupt subprime mortgage lenders, the closure of investment funds, and the strong market shocks caused by this. It resulted in a liquidity crisis facing the world's major financial markets. The US subprime mortgage market caused US interest rates to increase and led to continued cooling of the housing market.

Where does capitalism go from here? How can the financial system survive? Will the United States enter recession due to this? These questions were all considered by economists around the world. They were also asked of America's first black president.

The financial crisis forced the United States to reflect on its economic growth, raising the notion of 'deleveraging', and returning to a 'reindustrialization' strategy. In 2012, in his State of the Union address, President Obama used the word 'manufacturing' eight times. His predecessor, George W. Bush only mentioned the term once in eight addresses. Obama suggested that the American renaissance lay first and foremost in the revival of manufacturing, because manufacturing industry is the source of innovation. The American 'reindustrialization' process was not a retread of the traditional development of modern industry, rather it related closely to IT, and utilized Internet innovation to promote manufacturing innovation. With the big data backdrop, GE's CEO even proposed the concept of an 'Industrial Internet'.

After World War II the prevalence of global integration made it increasingly difficult to retain American manufacturing jobs. But with the help of the Internet, all aspects of manufacturing, from product design and production to sales and services were undergoing huge changes. The main effect was to make it easier to go from the idea to the final product. The upgrade cycle for each product was shortened, so while earlier cycles were a few months, this fell to a matter of weeks; what is more, local production has huge cost advantages.

Currently, the US has one of the lowest labour costs in the industrialized world. Boston Consulting Group released a report showing that in the United States per unit labour costs have fallen from $17.10 in 2006 to $9.20 in 2014. The report predicted that this would fall further to $6.90 in 2015. Part of the reason is the substantial increase in the productivity of Americans, but it is mainly because real wages have not changed, whereas in China, real wages have risen. In addition, American energy costs are the lowest among developed countries, mainly due to the American oil and shale gas revolution. The Federal Reserve noted that the energy advantage has prompted a three per cent increase in manufacturing output since 2006, investment has increased by ten per cent and the employment level increased by two per cent. Manufacturing was obviously returning to the United States, so globalization is pointing, to a certain extent to 're-Americanization'.

In this context, 3D printing technology in industries such as fashion, film, and architecture shows strong growth potential, and this has hugely changed the pattern of US manufacturing. With 3D printers, one can produce a one-off prototype. The new generation of intelligent manufacturing technology has lowered the thresholds for product design and manufacturing, and the desire to rapidly respond to the market and seize the opportunities has become the driving force of the new technology.

The use of robotics, cheap energy, product manufacturing, and technology research and development have become interdependent industry trends, and this change is becoming the focus of the new era of manufacturing. Information, energy-saving, new energy, and high value-added advanced manufacturing have become the expanded frontiers of manufacturing.

World-leading appliance manufacturing country

From 2002 to 2011, Chinese industry expanded rapidly, and the country became one of the world's leading appliance manufacturing countries. In 2002, the output of China's household electrical appliance industry had a value of ¥269.12 billion. By 2011, it had reached ¥1.1425 trillion, a 4.2-fold increase since 2002. In November 2001, China's accession to the WTO meant that the Chinese home appliance industry extended from competing only on the domestic market to covering the global market, providing a powerful impetus for the rapid development of the industry. In 2002, Chinese home appliance industry exports reached $8.75 billion; in 2011 they reached $47.23 billion, an increase of a factor of 4.4. In 2009, Chinese home appliance exports were 30 per cent of the global export market for home appliances. A number of global appliance giants built research and development centres in China, meaning that the Chinese home appliance industry developed distinctive international characteristics.

Over 10 years, China's home appliance industry made breakthroughs in a number of key areas, not only building a batch of internationally influential brands, but also cultivating a group of excellent professional and technical personnel. The Chinese home appliance industry has an outstanding record in air-cooled, multidoor refrigerator design and manufacturing technology, large capacity drum type washing machine design and manufacturing technology, and efficient air conditioning manufacturing technology and other aspects of technical research and development.

After the global financial crisis in 2008, as the state stimulated domestic demand with countryside appliance policies, trading old for new appliance policies and many other incentives, the Chinese home appliance industry expanded production capacity. In 2010, Haier invested in the construction of a refrigerator production base in Chongqing with an annual capacity of more than 2 million units. In March 2011, Haier announced that it would invest in the construction of a refrigerator manufacturer in Shenyang with an annual output of more than 2 million units, and also invest in the construction of a manufacturer of energy-saving and environmentally friendly freezers in Foshan, Guangdong Province, with an annual output of 2 million units. Early in March, Haier announced that it would invest ¥690 million in the technological transformation of a production base in Hefei producing three million units of energy-saving environmentally friendly refrigerators. The annual production capacity of Haier's Hefei refrigerator production base reached six million units, making it the world's largest single refrigerator production base. Later in March, Haier invested millions in Sanshui Market Innovation Industrial Park, in Foshan, which will have 300 million units of annual production capacity for drum washing machines.

While the Chinese home appliance production capacity for

many products accounts for the vast majority of global production, Chinese household electrical appliance enterprise involvement in the overseas market is still limited to the OEM segment, always surviving at the end of the industrial value chain, at the bottom of the smiling curve. (This is an illustration of the value-adding potential of different components of the value chain in an IT-related manufacturing industry. Both ends of the value chain command higher values added to the product than the middle part of the value chain. If this phenomenon is presented in a graph with a Y-axis for value-added and an X-axis for value chain – stage of production – the resulting curve looks like a smile.) Since 2001, the overseas business of Chinese home appliances has moved into the fast lane of development, and many export enterprises have maintained double-digit growth every year. But, apart from a very few companies such as Haier, more than 90 per cent of household electrical appliance exports are OEM and ODM (original design manufacturers – companies that design and manufactures products as specified eventually to be rebranded by another firm for sale), so they do not own their brands, have not established sales networks in overseas markets, and are unable to develop personalized products for overseas consumers.

Prior to 2008, the large chain retail giants had almost a monopoly on sales of appliances; Gome and Suning had made meteoric rises, changing the retail landscape of the 1990s appliance industry which had previously relied on regional agencies for product distribution. Household appliance enterprises, once caught up in the conflict of chain stores and self-owned channels, were unable to extricate themselves. In 2008, founder Liu Qiangdong decided that JD Mall had accumulated sufficient strength in the field of IT to enable him to open a home appliance purchasing network. This heralded a new era of diversified channels for the sale of home appliances, with a number of appliance companies announcing the expansion of their own distribution networks and Haier launching Goodaymart.

In the three years from 2008 to 2011, the implementation of the Countryside Policy for Home Appliances greatly expanded the demand for home appliances in tier 3 and 4 cities nationwide (in China tier 3 and 4 cities are smaller and less affluent, and are geographically dispersed). More importantly, the tier 3 and 4 market sales channel network was greatly expanded. For Haier, for example, by the end of 2010, county-level expansion included nearly 6,000 Haier Stores and 700 franchised Goodaymart malls. In the rural markets the company expanded into 28,000 sales outlets. This represented a doubling of the number of outlets compared to 2009, providing nationwide coverage of 80 per cent of towns and villages. At the same time, the previously entrenched large chain-store channels in first-tier cities began to move downwards, competing for the market in tier 3 and 4 cities. For example, at the end of 2010, there were more than 900 Suning stores in first and second tier markets, accounting for about 70 per cent of the total number of stores, while the stores targeting the tier 3 and 4 markets in towns and villages accounted for only 30 per cent. As large chains moved downwards, and the tier 3 and 4 chain store channels began to rise, household electrical appliance enterprises expanded their own channels meaning that the competition among the home appliances channels in tier 3 and 4 markets became more intense.

In the first and second tier markets, Internet channels like JD Mall have grown explosively, and although small overall, they have become a force to be reckoned with among the channels. Faced with a strong competitive pressure, Gome and Suning moved towards the field of electronic commerce, with Suning announcing, 'We cannot leave the huge cake of e-commerce to our competitors.' In addition, the home improvement building materials market is highly concerned about household electrical appliance enterprises and it is hoped that in the future this will become another main retail channel.

The home appliance channels are varied and diversified, so for Chinese home appliance enterprises, the effective combination of multiple channels and in-depth management of channel marketing has become a key issue, as the slightest mistake can lead to a crisis.

Second largest economy

In early 2011, the Japanese Cabinet Office released data showing that Japan's nominal GDP in 2010 was $5.4742 trillion, $404.4 billion less than that of China. This meant that China had officially passed Japan to become the world's second largest economy. Japan's post-Second World War economic miracle had ended.

By 1978, 30 years since the Chinese Economic Reform, the Chinese annual growth rate of gross national product reached 9.8 per cent. This number is comparable to that of Japan (9.2 per cent) and South Korea (8.5 per cent) during their economic take-off stages. Only seven countries (regions) have continued to increase at a rate of more than seven per cent annual growth for more than 30 years; China is one of them, and has the largest economy of them all.

The main cause of China's rapid growth was foreign trade and foreign investment. Looking at the development of Japan and the Asian tigers (South Korea, Singapore, Hong Kong and Taiwan), China abandoned the Soviet heavy industry development model in 1949, moving instead to a light industry and export-oriented development strategy. This eventually caused China's foreign exchange reserves to rank first in the world.

Chinese economic reform has greatly enhanced the level of national income and education. Looking at China's per capita income, whether in urban or rural areas, the quadrupling of GDP Deng Xiaoping wanted has been achieved. According to World Bank criteria, China has jumped from being one of the world's low-income countries to a middle-income country. At the same time, its economic growth has taken 140 million rural residents into the process of industrialization, enabling them to migrate to the cities. In terms of the industrial structure, China has transitioned from an industrial and agricultural economy to an industrial and commercial economy. Large enterprises were regularly emerging and grew rapidly. The 2007 list of Fortune 500 companies, included 22 mainland Chinese companies.

However, these remarkable economic achievements, directly

or indirectly created a variety of problems. For example, during the rapid development process, due to weak legislation or local government neglect, very serious environmental pollution was created. In another example, as Deng Xiaoping said, reform allows some people to get rich before others – 30 years later, some people are certainly rich, but other people's lives have not yet improved.

A Foreign Ministry spokesman said that although China has made remarkable achievements in economic development, the fact that it is still a developing country has not changed. The basic national conditions of China are still the same as those of a country in the primary stage of socialism. 'We have a clear understanding of this,' said the spokesman.

A number of issues have been seen by many economists as obstacles to China's sustained economic growth, including the investment to GDP ratio being too high, with about 50 per cent of GDP used for accumulation, there is insufficient consumption, or we could say that the labour income share of GDP is too small, and there is a high dependence on exports, etc. Despite this, there are still experts who predict that China will overtake the United States to become the world's largest economy.

Japanese and American companies make offensive and defensive moves

$5.6 billion, $4.7 billion and $9.8 billion: these were the 2011 losses of Japanese electronics giants Sony, Sharp and Panasonic. The $20 billion in total worth of losses marks the fact that the heyday of Japanese electronics companies has passed.

Richard Katz, editor of *Oriental Economist Report*, a journal looking at Japanese–American economic relations, pointed out that Japan's electronics exports in 2000 accounted for 26 per cent of total exports, but by 2011 this had fallen to 14 per cent. Electronics is no longer a significant source of trade for Japan.

Sony, Panasonic, Hitachi and other companies focused a lot of attention on tapes, portable music players and analogue TV, thereby missing the PC digital revolution of the late 1980s. And these companies then failed to react quickly enough to the rise of mobile devices.

The 2003 range of Sony products was far better than Apple's range, so why did the company fail to seize the opportunity to conduct product integration with the Internet? Precisely because the company's previous strong business model and successful experience generated conflicts of interest with digitalization and the adoption of the Internet, hindering the pace of innovation. That is, the more successful an enterprise, the more complacent they become. Too many businesses fall into the 'success trap'.

There were many other reasons for the decline of Japanese companies: they were overconfident about their own skills and manufacturing capabilities, while ignoring the user's perspective on their products; they were satisfied with incremental innovation and lacked the courage for destructive innovation; they didn't recognize the importance of software, and did not know how to integrate hardware and software; and the product line was too long, resulting in a blurred focus, and lack of direction.

On the other hand, since the start of the 1990s, the once defeated American companies slowly regained dominance. Why were American companies able to make a comeback within ten short years? Zhongshan University management professor Mao Yunshi believes that there are profound economic, technical and institutional reasons for this.

New enterprises are spawned by risk

Japanese venture capital firms are mainly held by banks, insurance companies and large enterprises, and they tend to prefer less risky investments, so the level of investments in start-ups (companies created less than five years ago) is just 16 per cent of the portfolio. Looking at the situation in the US, in contrast, 90 per cent or more venture capital firms are owned by independent enterprises, even general non-financial institutions and individuals are actively involved in venture capital activities. More than half of the funding comes from pension funds. American venture capital has a greater appetite for investment in start-ups and high-tech enterprises, and so obtains higher yields. The makeup of their investments includes 30 per cent start-ups, double the number in Japan. Investment in computer hardware and software, biotechnology, pharmaceuticals, telecommunications and other industries accounted for about 90 per cent of the total amount. More importantly, the United States has a sound risk investment system, providing not only ongoing financial assistance to start-ups and growing ventures, but also comprehensive technical, management, marketing, financing and listing support.

Corporate restructuring brings established businesses back to life

Corporate restructuring is a corrective for the over-expansion, and excessive diversification of the 1960s and 1970s, and is a strategic response made by a business to the changing environment. Since the 1980s, many US enterprises, especially large ones, have launched a sustained reconstruction process. During that time one in three of America's largest 1,000 companies has undergone some kind of corporate restructuring. The reconstruction of these large enterprises enabled them to overcome the 'big company disease' issues they faced. By daring to reduce business scope, consolidating the organization, optimizing core technology and raising the enterprise's core value they were able to resolve their existential crises. In Japan, economic development has slowed significantly since the 1980s, and although Japanese companies face a severe crisis of survival due to the economic and political system, constraints and management models, business philosophy of the enterprise and corporate governance structures and other factors, the appetite for reconstruction has been much weaker than in American companies. Government intervention and penetration of enterprises, cross-shareholdings between banks and enterprises, lifetime employment systems and the lack of focus on business profits are serious impediments to change for Japanese companies.

The use of information technology improves the competitiveness of enterprises

With the information technology revolution since the 1980s, technical development and equipment investment have been the dominant business trends. Almost all companies have established their own internal computer networks, and this connects with the regional, national and transnational networks, allowing rapid information processing, transfer and sharing. Through information investment in American manufacturing, major changes were made in production systems, inventory management, marketing systems, the development of products and services, business processes and improving labour productivity, all of which helped in regaining competitiveness. In comparison, Japanese companies missed a full ten years of the IT economy. By that time almost all the core IT of the economy was in the hands of the Americans. IT has formed an economic circle in which Japanese enterprises have no place.

The traditional Japanese management model is limiting

Japanese corporate management in the 1980s was a role model for the world economy and management community, but dramatic changes occurred in the external environment in the 1990s, and the rigid and slow-moving elements of the Japanese business management model limited its growth. For example, the personnel and payroll systems, along with Japan's lifetime employment system and the wage-seniority system, although beneficial to the stability and long-term development of the employees, also limits competition between employees in a way that is not conducive to large-scale technological innovation. More importantly, in an economic downturn, the traditional lifetime employment and business thinking hindered the survival of the businesses by preventing the use of layoffs and other means of improving finances, reducing the ability of the companies to withstand risks and recession. On the contrary, US companies directly link wages with duties, responsibilities and performance, and this encourages internal competition and an innovative business culture. At the same time, the number of employees increases or decreases with changes in the economic environment, making these enterprises better able to withstand recessions. Another example is the method used for decision-making and the exchange of views. Japanese companies emphasize consensus, so the decision-making process is slow. Although, once the decision is made it is executed relatively smoothly, this process is difficult to adapt to the new economy and the fast-changing market environment. On the other hand, American corporate decision-making is fast. Although there may be different views within the enterprise about the best decision, they can make a timely response and strategic adjustments for the market environment.

Treating 'big company disease' – 1,000-day reconstruction

Like Huawei and Lenovo, after 20 years of development, Haier had developed into a large international company. But it had never achieved a business structure, organizational structure, personnel structure or corresponding processes to match the scope of international companies. Haier Group had developed to a new critical point.

Haier's reconstruction, which started in 1998, and lasted nearly ten years, did not solve the above problem as the goal of that process had been to establish a set of operating systems for procurement, sales and so on, and to avoid conflicts after diversification. But, what was formed had its own problems – such as not really being connected to the market, resource waste and information distortion.

At that time, Haier was fragmented, and its 600 small computer systems could not be effectively integrated, so a series of 'information islands' were formed. When the business model changed, these small systems had to be abandoned. Zhang Ruimin was painfully aware that Haier had undergone several years of reconstruction without going far enough: 'Walking around you could see that it did have some effect, but it did not bring about the desired integration of information within the enterprise.' Therefore, starting from 26 April 2007, Haier launched a period of information technology reconstruction lasting 1,000 days, with the intention of creating 2000–2,500 processes.

This 1,000 Day Revolution included organizational, process and personnel reconstruction. In terms of the organization, Haier wanted to build an operationally excellent business. The idea was to take Haier's original information systems, which were distributed among different processes, and link them into an organic whole, so that all links in the chain were connected to the same, single goal which was that they could respond quickly to market requirements. In terms of personnel, the goal was to provide a way to enhance quality in an open environment, allowing collaboration and communication on information platforms, so that Haier staff could bring their energy and capability to the fore. The system was designed to maximize speed and accuracy, so that top talent could ensure operational excellence.

Zhang Ruimin says: 'This reconstruction was not the same as the previous attempts. The idea was to embed information technology into the entire system.' Haier invested hundreds of millions to change the enterprise, to allow a reconstruction based around information technology. In three years it had built up a comprehensive and innovative information processing and organizational system.

This allowed information to flow throughout the entire process, so that the system could respond immediately to events. Any customer demand or sign of trouble would be instantly fed back through every aspect of the process. If a new market order was raised, the order requirements would be instantly reflected throughout all sectors from marketing, research and development, supply, manufacturing, financial, human resources, etc., allowing simultaneous action throughout the entire chain, while also integrating resources. The system would automatically create a project to complete the order. This meant that orders could be met in the shortest possible time. In this process, everything became automatic. Because there were pre-budget processes, a 'zero signature' system could be achieved; because of the internal closed-loop process, it was possible to have a 'zero approval' system; and since the process was close to the market, it was also possible to achieve 'zero delays'. The entire process system may seem complicated to outsiders, but for customers, it was the easiest system to deal with.

This complex system is not a split execution process, but an instant process implemented jointly throughout the company. This means that customer demand and order objectives are clear, so the goods do not stay in storage and finances flow in the fastest way possible. It is an end-to-end system. Zhang Ruimin had stipulated that: 'Reconstruction must be objective and results-oriented; the criterion for the reconstruction is to build a process that works from target to target, from user to user, from end to end.'

In August 2007, Haier computers won an exclusive international tender for a Macedonian government computer project. When the prototype needed urgent revision, Haier's innovative internationalization process platform played a key role. Haier's Intel Product Innovation Centre, as well as the R&D centres in Germany, South Korea and Chinese Taiwan all started work at the same time. The design was quickly sent to the world's most outstanding manufacturing enterprises and prototype design changes were completed in the fastest possible time. This immediate response process meant that Haier took home orders of up to $30 million.

Process as the rudder

In Zhang Ruimin's original market chain theory there is a key concept known as 'creating a process with variable functions'. After 1998, 'process' was probably the most frequently heard word at Haier.

In the 1990s, Business Process Re-engineering originator Michael Hammer predicted that processes would be crucial for the twenty-first century and that excellent processes would enable successful companies to distinguish themselves from their competitors.

Businesses are often divided according to functional departments such as marketing, purchasing, production and finance. Initially each division in the company used IT technology to support its own processes, each had its own database and applications. However, customer orders pass through various parts of the organization. Customers issue orders to the sales department, this order is then transferred to the purchasing department and production department, finally, the financial department settles with the customer. Ideally, the business process merges the functions of different sectors together according to the customer requirements.

American entrepreneur Barry Diller has said that the longer he is engaged in business, the more he feels that the process is the most important thing. Process is the actual work you have done to translate a concept into a truly useful reality. He warns that without business processes, things become subject to accidental movement.

For Zhang Ruimin, processes are not only necessary requirements for the customer economy, but are the tool that allows strategic thinking to be implemented throughout the entire enterprise. He made several attempts to treat process like the rudder on a ship, changing the entire course of the Haier Group.

Before the 1,000 Day Revolution, Haier's business flowchart saw two big changes. The first was putting order information at the centre of the system, completely separating the original finance, procurement and sales operations divisions, integrating them and forming commercial development headquarters, logistics development headquarters and cash flow headquarters. This brought about the unification of sales, purchasing and billing throughout the whole group. This is the main process behind the Haier market chain. The original functional management processes were integrated, so that they were registered as independent operational service companies forming an innovative order support process known as the 3Rs (R&D, HR development and CR [customer relationship management]). The 3Rs ensure complete implementation of the order (*dan*) on the basis of the 3T supporting processes (TCM, total cost management; TPM, total productive maintenance; and TQM, total quality management). All these were built on two very important foundations: the Haier corporate culture and information management systems.

During the 1,000 Day Reconstruction the original functional structure of Haier was turned into a process-oriented network; the vertical business was transformed into a horizontal business. Several key processes were redesigned, including commercial development, logistics and cash flow, with the goal of speeding up the response rate of the global supply chain. In logistics, for example, Haier's original procurement division, warehousing and distribution of raw materials, finished goods warehousing and distribution, which had been divided among 28 products, were unified, optimizing external resources through the integration of the internal resources. The main tasks of the product division follow the three elements of quality, cost and delivery requirements (in that order), so that production of products meets consumer demand. Under this new system, which directly faces the market with unified logistics, commercial development, and capital flow, Haier's original management departments lost their administrative functions, becoming support processes instead.

In 2004, the business flowchart changed once again. In addition to Haier's core processes, four management processes were added for strategic planning, operational reporting, internal audit and IT management. Below these are the total quality management, total productive maintenance, total cost management, and cultural and human resources management processes. Compared with the previous flow chart, the basic requirement, as always, is to move order (*dan*) information to the centre, as the driving force behind logistics and cash flow. That is, only after valuable orders are obtained from the market (reaching Haier margin requirements), can the logistics and capital flow begin operations around the order. The logistics deliver the product to the customers, and cash flow returns the payments from customers. Since production occurs only for an order, after products enter the workflow, cash can be immediately raised for the goods. Haier refers to these as 'core processes'.

An additional four management processes were then added, reflecting the importance Zhang Ruimin attaches to budget rigidity. For most Chinese enterprises budgets are equivalent to targets, and goals are specific numbers. For example, if the overall objective of the Group is 1 billion or 2 billion, this would be broken down, with specific numbers being given to particular divisions and targets being executed in accordance with this. However, there is potentially nothing behind the budgets. Haier now requires that targets must be systematic, goals must be competitive, and at the same time, it must be made clear what resources are needed to support the achievement of the objectives. In addition, there should also be a link between the reward and punishment mechanism and results. After the flow chart was changed, Haier no longer allowed budgets to be simple numbers; for example, how much should be completed in a certain year. Instead, the focus was on what was used to complete the targets. In this way the number from the budget is turned into a type of competition.

For managers at Haier, implementation of the four management processes can be a challenge. A vice president once said he felt that things became more difficult under the new flow chart: if the target he raised did not meet the stipulations for the growth of the Haier Group, he would not get it passsed; but if it were too high it would still not pass the test, because he would also have to demonstrate what resources would be required to support the achievement of such high growth. Zhang Ruimin's request was tantamount to forcing the company objectives onto the shoulders of each individual: 'In the past, rigid budgets were used to make decisions,' he explained, 'now the number of orders and contracts we receive is what we care about. This is where the rigidity lies. So it is no longer a game between me and you, but between you and the market.'

In this flow chart we see the emergence of PLM (product

lifecycle management), SCM (supply chain management), CRM (customer relationship management) and SRM (supplier relationship management). During the 1,000 Day Reconstruction, these processes were subjected to an unprecedented strengthening.

The ERP detour

At midnight on 1 January 2008, after a long and arduous preparation, Haier Group's ERP system HGVS (Haier Global Value System) went online. The HGVS system was the largest, most complex ERP integration project in the history of Haier. One of the core objectives was to achieve visualization. Prior to this, orders from the frontline could not be seen by Haier suppliers, which resulted in a long supply chain. The company could not guarantee fast supply, because the suppliers could not see Haier's planning system. This was a problem advanced manufacturing companies such as Hewlett-Packard had already resolved – all vendors see the whole situation at the same time as Hewlett-Packard.

To pass jobs through the entire system requires common coding and integration. Visual management does not consider business management from the IT point of view, but considers business issues from a business perspective. In R&D, for example, if visualization is performed well, Haier's global designers are able to work together on the same design drawings, because they all have access to the blueprint and are able to modify the master copy. After modification, samples can be produced.

Haier had high hopes for the development of HGVS, and invested heavily. However, issues appeared very quickly. Zhang Ruimin recalls: 'There was a period of time when we used the ERP system for marketing, and sales plummeted. After just a few months, it was like paralysis. The structure had not changed, but we had created a new process, and the two did not match … the original creation of ERP in isolation could only create a situation where the staff and system were like oil and water. Only after adding some additional thinking could we combine the two properly.'

This meant that the Haier reconstruction process took a detour, because the best process is one, which has the shortest distance from the customer. Zhang Ruimin reflects on this:

While engineering the process, we initially thought the original attempt was unsuccessful due to the poor construction process, so as soon as we started reconstruction based around ERP, we listed thousands of processes. We spent quite a lot of money both for hardware and for software, and everything regarding the process was done well, as we had invited an international consulting firm. However, looking at the process–market connection we suddenly realized that this approach was not acceptable. We now believe that if processes are a necessary condition, the 'aligning individuals and goals' method would be a sufficient condition.

Zero inventory, instant supply as demand rises

Zhang Ruimin firmly believed that Haier's business model needed to move from 'selling stock' to 'zero inventory, instant supply as demand rises', so on 28 August 2008, Haier took the drastic step of eliminating central storage. This sounds like a paradox. If the customer has requirements, and there are no products in the inventory and warehouse, how can customer orders be fulfilled? On the other hand, if the customer has no requirements, how can Haier operate without producing stock? It was necessary to take the enterprise through an entire process. Previously, ERP was made unilaterally behind closed doors, but now the ERP was designed for customer management for the market. All Haier processes were required to meet the user's needs.

The term 'inventory' was redefined, so that it did not refer only to finished goods but also to inventory of semi-finished products and raw materials. This is akin to Toyota's JIT (just in time) system. The important aspect of this is that a complete and thorough understanding of the customer requirements is needed, and production predictions should be very accurate.

When promoting this model, Haier encountered a great deal of resistance. Front-line sales staff said that if we do this, we may not be able to sell many Haier products. Zhang Ruimin said: 'If they are not sold then we will stop producing. What should we do after we stop? Put pressure on our system to make necessary adjustments.' In fact, the change was not fully understood, either inside or outside the company, and there were some who thought that it was too radical and might lead to the downfall of the enterprise. Indeed, it was a big shock and led to Haier making losses. However, Zhang Ruimin did not back down; he believed that 'in the final analysis, the business model is supposed to maximize customer value'.

Instant supply when there is demand under the zero inventory framework forces the entire system to meet the needs of individual users, rather than being fragmented. In the event, this played a huge role in changing the organizational structure of Haier.

Haier persevered, and finally found a way. Appliance retail giants Suning and Gome started actively cooperating with Haier, and also asked other suppliers to supply goods in the same way as Haier. To accelerate cash flow, Haier's inventory turnaround was only five days, one-tenth of the average for China's home appliance industry, bringing about greatly reduced costs.

Haier began construction of the first franchised stores in 1996. In 1999, the Group set up its Commercial Development Headquarters, developing Haier's specialist stores; and in 2006, the company developed stores with the three characteristics of being concentrated (with big storefronts and distributions networks), professional and exclusive (only selling Haier products). The stores are not only sales centres but are also service centres and distribution centres. After nearly 20 years of development, Haier has more than 30,000 outlets throughout China, 8,000 county-level stores, and 23,000 township level stores.

In 2008, Haier established community stores in the residential compounds of first and second tier markets, and there are now more than 3,000. The company began to explore the integration of service and marketing and using services to win customer resources. At that time, large chain channels had a near monopoly, and while competitors had to rely on large chain stores, Haier was able to use its own systems to sell directly to users, seamlessly meeting their needs. Combined with the zero inventory policy, this formed a fully integrated system, allowing the company to move from being enterprise-centric to focusing on the needs of the individual user.

As early as 2007, Haier began building Goodaymart malls outside the Haier specialist store system. The biggest difference between Goodaymart and the Haier store system was that Goodaymart malls include many appliance brands alongside Haier, as well as well-known IT products. Haier's aim was to create an open platform. So in terms of their sales volumes, although Haier's own business would still account for the majority, by about 2013, some 40 per cent of business would be accounted for by other suppliers. According to Haier's plans, in the following two years, the sales of other company's products were expected to exceed that of its own.

Today, the Goodaymart platform has established nationwide coverage from urban to rural areas including 30,000 shops, shipping bases, 90 distribution centres and a total storage area of more than 2 million square metres. At the same time, more than 7,600 stores have been established at county-level, along with around 26,000 town-level stores, and 19,000 village-level focal points. They have created a service network of more than 2,800 national county-level distribution stations and 17,000 service stations. There are 90,000 service vehicles, 80,000 service staff, and these people all live within the user's world, so they can provide users with a localized, face-to-face service. Goodaymart has created an integrated appliances and big-ticket goods warehousing, logistics, distribution and installation service network. Compared to other current large domestic logistics and distribution systems, Goodaymart has obvious advantages. The ultimate goal is to build an open service platform focused on home appliances, furniture, home improvement, household drinking water, family services and community services, matching the concept of 'Haier Smart Life'.

Since the plan started in 1996, Haier has invested more than ¥30 billion in channel construction. In 2011, for the development of e-commerce, Haier established another mall, offering 24-hour delivery, with free orders if they are late. Since the company's storage system has been dismantled, Haier is proud to say that by the time a customer places an order, the goods will already be on the road.

Independently managed operational bodies

After the ERP detour, Zhang Ruimin learned that processes and people must be fully integrated into a single unit. Three years after the 1,000 Day Reconstruction, in 2010, Zhang Ruimin clarified Haier's business model as being 'individual goals together and win-win models'. The specific content of the model can be described as a combination of real and virtual networks, featuring zero inventory and instant supply as demand arises'. In fact, this was a very difficult task to achieve as it was necessary to create a fast network, and also to have accurate information, so it had to be both fast and systematic. In Zhang Ruimin's words, the company was 'fighting against the habits of Chinese people'. This fight was not only a fight against the habits of employees, but also a fight against poor corporate culture. 'Enterprises must maintain transparent personal relationships, as well as equity, efficiency and stability.'

In 2010, in order to rapidly promote organizational change, the concept of independently managed autonomous bodies, unique in the global business community to Haier, and referred to using the Chinese acronym 'ZZJYT', was created. Haier's theoretical framework now finds organizational support.

ZZJYTs are the smallest internal business units at Haier. They could just be one individual, or a group of people. The essence of the idea was to turn the big company into thousands of small companies. These ZZJYTs are sometimes referred to simply as 'autonomous bodies'. They are the cells making up Haier's organization, and they number as many as 2,000. These ZZJYTs are not only able to respond rapidly to external changes, they are also able to discover and create customer demand – while also continually returning to value targets, without losing focus on the ultimate goal of meeting customer needs.

These 2,000 ZZJYTs form a big network directly facing the market. Each ZZJYT is like a node on this network, where each node can become a basic unit of innovation. Since these basic units of innovation are just like real companies they are given 'three powers' by the Group: decision-making, distribution rights and the right to use human resources.

Haier also developed the concepts of benefit sharing bodies (known as LGTs) and platforms. LGTs refer to a community having the same interests. LGTs are, to a degree, an extension of the ZZJYTs, in that ZZJYTs, external suppliers and partners and other stakeholders together form an LGT. Each LGT can come together or separate as required according to the changing conditions so as to bring about their value and create synergies.

In practice, LGTs are often several ZZJYTs joined together, but the leader of an LGT does not play a leadership role, rather, he or she is an initiator. LGTs are like a small platform, and Haier is working towards the idea of moving the entire business onto a large platform.

Platforms are a way to quickly configure resources, while all resources can be deployed through the platform. The goal is for the organization to become self-organized rather than something organized by others. Zhang Ruimin believes that, 'The organization should never take orders from someone else, but should self-organize and innovate itself.'

The self-organization's ultimate measure is to be propelled by orders, with better people coming in, producing better results, and obtaining higher profits, then introducing more good people. As Peter Drucker said, the end result is that everyone becomes their own CEO.

This process drives a virtuous cycle following the principle of increasing returns, and was the ultimate goal of pursuing the networked organization. In the industrial economy, success is often self-limiting, as it follows the principle of diminishing returns. However, in the network economy, success is self-reinforcing, and follows the principle of increasing returns.

Changing the direction of the game

Haier has many ways of talking about the ZZJYTs. The most common interpretation for them starts by looking at the 'three criteria': end to end, the same goal, forced system. Here, 'end to end' refers to the front-line managers starting from the customer, and ending by meeting the needs of the customer, so the process both starts from, and ends with, the client. 'The same goal' refers to the situation after goals are set, when they are no longer personal goals, but rather all team members work together to achieve the shared goal of meeting customer needs. The 'forced system' refers to the situation in which the user's requirements are the goal, and this is forced onto all the internal processes of Haier. This is done following the principle of 'turning over sufficient corporate profits, earning sufficient marketing fees, self-financing all ZZJYT activities, and splitting excessive profits after all these are done'. Everyone has their own financial statement, and everyone has calculations applied to them, so now the tens of thousands of workers at the company are effectively running their own finances.

Another way to talk about it is the 'three-selfs': self-innovation, self-running, and being self-driven. Again, ZZJYTs are ultimately self-organizing. Self-innovation is used to find a strategy and set the corresponding objectives; being self-driven refers to finding the path to implement the strategy and achieve the goals; self-running refers to the construction of independent systems and optimized goals. The three are interconnected and complement each other. Finally, self-organization will be achieved, which means that in the chaotic external environment, the self-organizing body can sense changes occurring outside, and respond appropriately.

In order to motivate employees to self-organize, Haier created a special class of AB employees, who are capable of creating, innovating, self-driving, and self-operating without guidance, continually creating AB class products and users. AB products are those which both create value for the user and give the enterprise high added value; class AB users are loyal Haier customers and would recommend the company to others.

Wharton management professor Marshall Meyer conducted a research project at Haier, with a particular focus on the essence of the ZZJYTs. He analysed the company's contract system, that is, the way the company is defined as a combination of a series of contracts, in which contracts can occur between the enterprise and the external market, but can also occur internally within the enterprise, with the key relationship being that between the principal and the agent.

Meyer found that ZZJYTs are a kind of method for competitive bidding with the winners being whoever best achieves the objectives and targets. These objectives are then connected to remuneration. He also found that ZZJYT evaluations are not measured by sales, but in terms of market share and earnings, as well as metrics including new product development, customer satisfaction, and so on. His most significant finding was that the contract between Western enterprises and agents is static, and will not change after being signed, whereas in Haier's ZZJYT management model, the contract is subject to dynamic adjustments. Haier does not have a simple principal-agent relationship with its ZZJYTs.

The traditional principal-agent relationship can be seen as one example of game theory being applied between the principal and agent. In the first stage, the client provides a mechanism arrangement. The second stage is that the agent decides whether to accept such a mechanism; if he refuses, nothing will happen, if the mechanism is accepted, then they enter the third stage of the game. In the third stage, the agent, under the framework of constraint of the mechanism, selects the most favourable action for themselves. However, this is precisely the gaming Zhang Ruimin wanted to circumvent. If the enterprise applied a non-cooperative 'policies are implemented from above, and measures are implemented from below' game, the enterprise could lose, while the employees would win; or the enterprise could win, while the employees lost. But either way, it is impossible to achieve a win-win situation. What ZZJYTs do is to take the game between employees and businesses, and change it so that satisfying user requirements becomes a game with oneself.

Zhang Ruimin told Professor Meyer:

Haier's ZZJYTs are hugely different from the structures used at Western companies. In essence it is the creation of contracts between businesses and consumers. What users require is what must be satisfied, rather than where there are contracts within the enterprise. Stated another way, the internal contract is there to meet the requirements of users, and between the users. We are a user-oriented enterprise, whereas Western companies are enterprise-centric enterprises.

The idea of the 'dynamic contracts' is that all the ZZJYTs work does not fulfil the instructions given by the corporation, but rather it has to be subjected to the user's requirements.

Zhang Ruimin – All employees work on contracts

We are in pursuit of all-employee contracts for the Internet era, so everyone is an entrepreneur. Drucker said that in tomorrow's information-intensive organizations, the vast majority of people will be managing themselves. In the information age, an enterprise should allow everyone to be their own CEO. This was one of the goals of our business, and our ZZJYTs exist to allow employees to operate independently.

What is different in the way we operate compared to the way American companies operate? American enterprises run principal-agent incentive contracts. In these contracts, the principals are shareholders, and the agents are professional managers. The principals give options to the agents, so they make profit from the options, and enterprises can only move upwards when they bring about the user's expected value, and only when the value increases can the stock options be cashed. So, the principal-agent incentive contracts provide extremely strong motivation. However, although the principal-agent incentive contracts are very good, they are only working for a small number of people. Our 'individual orders together' system is targeted at everyone, so we have an all-employee contract.

Why must we do this? Because if you do not subvert the system it is easy to get 'big business disease'. John Forbes Nash posited that there is a non-cooperative game equilibrium. If everyone is seeking to maximize their own interests, they will form a status quo in which 'you have a policy, so I will create a counter policy'. It is better to reverse the situation, and let participants play the game for their own interests. If this is not done, then staff would engineer small profits at the expense of the growth or survival of the whole enterprise.

Goal-oriented recruitment and dismissal – mutual selection of team leaders and members

In the individual orders together and ZZJYT framework, Haier's executive power resides in a combination of three elements – objective/group/mechanism, that is, what mechanisms to use, what kind of team to set up, and how to reach the 'leading' goals. Reaching the goals is paramount.

'Leading' is a common term used in Haier's strategic vision. In the Haier system employees are encouraged to think, 'what others cannot do, I will do, and I will do it using Internet methods'. For enterprises like Haier, which have come through the Internet era, the challenge of 'leading' is considerable. It is a bit like the stretched goals advocated by Jack Welch at GE. That is, in order to bring about change, almost unattainable goals and targets are set.

ZZJYTs bring about two elements of self-organization: the introduction of negative entropy and a positive feedback loop. 'Negative entropy' means constantly bringing in better human resources. Haier is currently exploring the establishment of an 'individuals meeting and parting' human resources platform: the staff are not fixed, and employees, customers, and suppliers meet and part on one single platform. Once the project is determined, according to the project objectives, the best human resources to do it are convened. These resources may be internal Haier resources, or could be external to Haier. The team only remains together until the completion of the project, meaning that when moving onto the next project, the resource requirements are reassessed.

The second element is the 'positive feedback loop'. This can be expressed in eight Chinese characters: 竞单上岗，官兵互选 'competition for the posts, when team leaders and members are mutually selected'. 'Competition for the posts' means that those who have the required abilities will compete to undertake the project. The main reason for 'big company disease' is the calcification of layers; if the manager has no energy, then the employees have no hope. Haier allows all employees to compete to become the head of the ZZJYT. But after the competition, the position is not held forever. If, during the process, the ZZJYTs do not reach the intended targets, and the members of the body believe the leadership to be responsible for the failure, they can start a recall procedure and select a new leader. However, conversely, the leadership can also decide to dismiss a member of a ZZJYT.

Zhang Ruimin says 'people across the world can be managed by our Human Resources Division'. He would like to build a networked organization through a goals-based platform, with individuals meeting and parting, bringing together the world's top resources on demand at any time. Not only can this achieve operational excellence, but it also greatly expands the boundaries of the enterprise. Haier vice president Diao Yunfeng is responsible for an international trading firm which is totally run by a team consisting of 'individuals meeting and parting'. Projects in Nigeria and Venezuela were given to one leader, but this leader organized resources from around the world to come together in a virtual team, so the individuals can meet to work on the project and then part when it is successfully completed.

Zhang Ruimin believes that in the future, all large enterprises will be replaced by platform-oriented enterprises, which will be open systems that can integrate large quantities of resources.

Zhang Ruimin – Individuals who meet and part, and interfaces

In the past, employees were the recipients of instructions from managers, but now they have become interfaces (*jiekouren*) for resources. Interfaces do not operate in isolation, but by collecting more resources.

In the past, we were people working in our business, and if employees could not do their work, the company would do everything possible to ensure they could finish the tasks, but if an individual really could not do their tasks, there would be no way for the company to move forward. The situation has changed. We now focus on the global scope and pressure on the staff is very high, either you become a first-class resource, or you are eliminated. Of course, we are not saying you have to do it all by yourself – you can serve as an interface, interfacing with the world's first-class resources.

For example, at one point we had 1,100 people working on research and development. Now we don't need that resource because we can go to MIT for assistance. A lot of the world's leading resources are servicing us. Today, this interface's resources extend to encompass more than 50,000 people. This is many, many times larger than before, and still the number continues to expand.

'Goals-oriented recruitment and dismissal' platforms generate a multiplier effect. In the past we may have believed that, for example, if we sold 100 products one year, sales of 120 the next year would be good progress, but actually there may have been market space to sell 500. We could not grow that quickly in one burst, but now that we have a platform-based team, we can achieve integration with 600 human resources, so I can suddenly jump to 500 from less than 100; this is the multiplier effect I was talking about. The reason why we can achieve a multiplier effect is because we have the capacity to interact. In the past, we relied only on ourselves, and how much capacity could we have?

What happens if we disperse leadership so that it is not exclusive to management? Each node in the networked organization becomes an interface, and all nodes are able to marshal first-class resources to create value for users beyond expectations.

Thirty years of Haier

ZZJYTs

Zhao Feng is one of the most successful examples of a ZZJYT among the more than 2,000 at Haier. He runs a Haier Community Store ZZJYT, and is responsible for product sales and customer services. As the head of the ZZJYT, Zhao Feng manages more than 80 community stores operating in more than 1,000 residential areas in Qingdao.

There are clear differences in the operational model between the regional marketing companies of traditional enterprises and Haier's Qingdao community store management ZZJYT. The ZZJYT leader is not like the general manager of a branch, completing tasks following the instructions sent down by the higher powers, he is more like the boss of a company with market-linked operation, independent accounting and profit and loss responsibility.

Zhao Feng's income fluctuates from month to month as, just like a business owner, his income is entirely dependent on the profitability of the Qingdao stores and is based on sharing the value he creates for users. Zhao Feng has the same authority that a boss would have and he does not take orders from the company's management, but makes the operational policy for the ZZJYT according to user requirements.

Zhao Feng has transformed the stores he is responsible for into a number of ZZJYTs, allowing each to be managed by an individual who faces the market and users, and has autonomous decision-making. The standard used for deciding their revenue is the same as that used for Zhao Feng; it is determined by the operating revenue of their own community stores.

Another successful example is the refrigerator R&D ZZJYT. This 18-member R&D team research refrigerators. Its 2011 net income reached nearly a billion yuan. Pu Xiankai and the team members of this ZZJYT enjoy creating and sharing value, and also feel the pressure of 'being their own bosses'. 'In the past, R&D personnel just worked on product development, now our goal is to create a market. As long as we meet the first competitive goals, the team can share the benefits of the added value. I care not only about profit sharing, but more importantly, about individual and team growth,' Pu says.

Haier's three tables

At the core of the ZZJYT operating system are three distinct tables: the strategic income statement, daily clearing table and individual order and payment table. Haier believes that the strategic income statement is the foundation, determining strategic direction. The daily clearing table includes the strategic income statement, and is fed through to the individual order and payment table, allowing strategic corrections during the process. The individual order and payment table shows the success of the ZZJYT and its members in executing their strategy.

Strategic income statement – ZEUS

The ZZJYT strategic income statement is different in three ways from a traditional income statement: traditional income statements are guided by numbers, with the revenue minus costs and expenses equalling profit while strategic income statements are focused around the value for users. The content is divided into four quadrants and is known as the 'Zeus model.'

QUADRANT 1

The first quadrant represents end user resources or value, the ultimate goal is to achieve zero distance from the customer. There are two key phrases: user interaction and leading competitiveness. User interaction is a very big challenge for traditional enterprises. In the past the question for Haier was how to understand and create value for the user, but now things have changed and the users have become part of the business, participating in the company's product design. Interaction with users has become a part of the entire process. For example, when designing a new innovative product, the user is first involved by providing advice. They may not know how to do the actual design, but they can help Haier understand the perspective of users so it can provide what they need. After the design is complete more online interaction takes place. Through the interaction, these users become the final consumers. So, assessment indicators were implemented at Haier measuring the products on the production line in terms of how many would end up in the hands of users. Traditional enterprises produce products which are not made for any user, but which are manufactured for the warehouse. Now Haier ensures that they already know the target users for around 20 per cent of the products being produced. Of course, it hopes that this proportion can be further improved. This allows users to more actively participate in the design process.

The second key phrase is leading competitiveness. Haier allows users to participate because it hopes to lead the industry. The American disruptive innovation guru Clayton M. Christensen separates innovation into two levels, the first-level is sustaining innovation, referring to upgrading original products, the second level is disruptive innovation, where completely different and original products are created, leading the industry. Haier anticipates that interaction with the users finally results in disruptive innovation.

QUADRANT 2

The second quadrant is human resources. Entrepreneurial employees undertake the user interaction, and lead the objectives from the first quadrant. Haier used to be a big company just like anyone else, but now it is divided into more than two thousand ZZJYTs. Each ZZJYT creates value for its own users, and is not simply measured by a single number – a system that prevents cheating.

QUADRANT 3

The third quadrant represents processes, and talks about landing on the target, that is, there is zero distance between preset goals and the result, there should be zero gap between the budget and the actuals. The traditional income statement is a post-hoc analysis, whereas strategic income statements are pre-event budgets. The economic analysis for an enterprise looks at past data, calculating done deals. Haier now plans how to win in advance, analysing what work will be required to reach the objective.

Haier has a daily clearance system, which means the work for each day must be completed on the day. The daily work follows the principle of the 'three zeros'. The first zero is 'zero inventory' – as soon as a user requires a product, it must be provided immediately. The marketing staff initially resisted zero inventory because they felt it would be impossible, but it was gradually pushed through. After encountering problems and getting feedback from the market, marketing, design, manufacturing and other related processes combined together to meet user needs. The second principle is 'zero signatures'. Zhang Ruimin believes that signing documents is unnecessary because one task may require the signature of lots of people and after signing no one is responsible for pushing it through to the end. The third principle is 'zero redundancy'. That is, everyone should have their own users, if they do not have their own users, then they do not exist in the organizational sense.

QUADRANT 4

The fourth quadrant represents closing the gap and improving. This is a single person driving him or herself, allowing more capable people to produce higher orders and create user value, so they can share value with customers and employees.

Daily clearing table

Following from the strategic income statement, the daily clearing table is produced. One of the most difficult things when doing business is setting very high, very competitive targets early in the month, but finding a large way still to go before meeting them at the end of the month. The goal of daily clearing tables is to predict (calculate) the gap between the budget and the actual, ensuring that necessary work is completed every single day, so pre-emptive measures can be taken to prevent gaps, avoiding the issue of problems arising which cannot be resolved.

Individual order and payment table (ren dan chou biao)

The third table is the individual order and payment table, where the results of operations are directly applied to each person. The idea is that 'if I create value for my users, I can share the added value'. The individual order and payment table is focused on orders. These are not determined by internal factors but by the competitive market, and people need the competence to complete these orders. Salaries are linked to the final value created for the customer. Many companies, including Haier, offered fixed salary jobs in the past, but the concept of the individual order and payment table is that the income is not determined by rank, it is only related to the value created. Exactly as Peter Drucker said, a person who makes a significant contribution and is responsible for results, no matter how junior, is still considered a 'top manager'. And conversely, if senior managers are not held accountable for results, they are not truly top managers.

Zhang Ruimin – The 'two dimensional' lattice

The 'two-dimensional lattice', is specific to each person, and we use this chart to assess each employee. It has two axes, the horizontal one is the same as that used by various other businesses, with numbers reflecting sales, profits and so on, showing whether we are hitting the industry average, leading the industry or coming first in the industry. The main thing to note is that if a ZZJYT's sales income or profits are very good, but on the vertical axis it does not show that real customer value was created, these otherwise good numbers will not be recognized. The first section of the vertical axis breaks the numbers down to the level of individuals, and someone must be responsible for each of these numbers. The numbers on the horizontal axis were originally fragmented, there was a number for sales, and a number for R&D, but on the vertical axis, all numbers for all the processes have someone who is responsible for whether they are good or bad. The second section of the vertical axis shows everyone's added value on the horizontal line, so if someone realized a value of ¥1 million it would be shown here, but this ¥1 million must be a product of disruptive innovation, rather than through creating a standard product. If it is a standard product, then the value is lowered; that is, even if it causes growth, it is considered low value.

Energy management

Haier's strategic income statement is in line with the third phase of the development management theory described by Zhang Ruimin: the energy management stage. The first phase was physical administration, which as the name suggests was based around things rather than people, the most well known theory of this type is Taylor's scientific management theory. While improving production efficiency, it also means that people become auxiliaries to machines, and their initiative and creativity is eradicated. The most obvious method for solving this shortcoming in people management is the team spirit process applied by Japanese companies, for example, W. Edwards Deming's TQM. Japanese companies were able to take TQM to its extreme, greatly enhancing the competitiveness of their products. Japanese companies are no longer so competitive, and an important reason for this is that enterprises are entering the energy management stage. Its biggest feature is the core of innovation, which reflects the value of human capital, so the formerly managed employees become managers in specific fields.

Haier has one production line which once required 45 people, but was later streamlined to five people. By improving the quality of personnel, efficiency has been increased 10 times over. Modular production was introduced so that one module can be applied in 10 or 20 models.

Experiments like these show how energy management works. Improving quality is not restricted to how much the quality of individuals can be improved, but to the overall coordination of the system. In this term, 'energy' refers to 'ability', but with the information economy, the knowledge economy, and the rise of knowledge workers, the word energy has become closer in meaning to 'intelligence'. It refers to the use of open architecture, which allows the energy of the system to be liberated. Basically, the enterprise is truly linked with the outside world.

Obviously, Zhang Ruimin was deeply influenced by the 'third industrial revolution' theory. In this industrial revolution, driven by intelligent management, unmanned operation will become the next mainstream trend in manufacturing. To bring this about requires new technologies and ways of thinking such as open systems, cloud computing, big data, 3-D printing and so on, all of which are completely different from traditional methods.

In times of change all an organization can do is to maintain homeostasis. In the Internet era, the best balance is achieved through open systems, as open systems have active behavioural characteristics. They are like the free will of living bodies. In complexity theory this is known as positive feedback.

Zhang Ruimin's goal for Haier is to create a body, which lives and breathes with its customers. The ultimate state of this living body is that everyone is a micro-enterprise, and the Haier group uses contracts to bring together all the micro-enterprises, eventually forming an immense network.

This has similarities to a management philosophy put forward by Japanese author Kazuo Inamori in his book *Amoeba Management*, which describes businesses based on small departments managed and accounted individually, like the freely repeating cell division found in an amoeba. With the leaders of the amoeba as the core, they develop their own plans, and undergo continual autonomous growth so that every employee becomes a lead performer and active participant. However, Zhang Ruimin feels that an amoeba organization would encounter problems in the Internet era, because amoeba businesses still have a triangular structure and do not have a good grasp of the changing needs of users, so if managers send flawed instructions to their staff, there are problems throughout the organization. The biggest difference between the amoeba structure and Haier's ZZJYTs is that ZZJYTs create platforms and mechanisms to enable individuals to achieve understanding of the needs of users.

The ZZJYT model has already taken root within Haier, and many of the traditional functions of the manager have been rewritten. Now they are called 'ZZJYT Heads', 'Network Heads', and 'Interfaces'. These are all roles focused on the management of 'energy'.

Can ZZJYT be regarded as a Chinese style of management? Zhang Ruimin has said that Chinese enterprises learned from many Western management methods, but that these methods are only tools, and they are not Chinese management models. He believes that mechanisms are an important marker of whether an enterprise can continue sustained development and optimization. He researched Leonid Hurwicz's mechanism design theory, in particular the problem of incentive compatibility for which Hurwicz (jointly) won the 2007 Nobel Prize in Economics. Incentive compatibility means that within a designed framework, while each individual pursues their personal interests they can also reach the targets set by the designer.

Good mechanisms have two characteristics: participation constraint and incentive compatibility constraints. The mechanism means that people are not forced to participate where they are not willing or interested. This is the participation constraint. Incentive compatibility constraints mean connecting the interests of the collective and individual as closely as possible, so the work takes place under the precondition of maximizing both corporate and personal interests. Looking at these two mechanism standards, Zhang Ruimin felt that since China's economic reform the most suitable mechanism was the contract responsibility system:

During the era of people's communes, there was no participation constraint, but if you asked a farmer to go and work, he would not go, because there was no incentive compatibility. However, under the contract responsibility system even if you did not require the farmer to go to the field, they would go and work anyway, because there was incentive compatibility. First turned over to the state, then to the collective, the rest of the fruits of their labour were the farmer's own.

In practice, Haier's ZZJYTs use the slogan 'I create my users, so I can share in the added value', and here the shadow of mechanism design theory can be clearly seen.

The inverted triangle

Front-line staff have boldness and courage thanks to the flat network organization. In the past, Haier's organizational structure was a pyramid, with top leadership at the peak, followed by senior managers, managers and so on down to the lowest level employees; front-line employees simply obeyed instructions from their superiors. The adoption of the 'zero inventory, supply on demand' business model was a complete change, allowing employees to move from the bottom of the triangle to the top, allowing autonomous decision-making when directly facing the market and users. Those previously at the very top were moved to the very bottom, mainly so that they could search for new strategic opportunities, while optimizing cooperation within the organization. Functional departments were minimized, and from sending instructions, they were transformed to focusing on providing resources and services.

This change means that the customer is the leader rather than senior leadership, front-line staff make a commitment to customers, and the top leadership must provide resources and platforms to support them.

Zhang Ruimin had previously discussed this issue with former IBM CEO Lou Gerstner. He drew the shape of an inverted triangle on a piece of paper, Gerstner was immediately clear about it; he said that he had wanted to do that while at IBM, but there were two problems he worried about: first, once the top people directly face the market and find problems, if their supporters below do not provide timely support, it would create great trouble. It would be like fighting without a good supply of ammunition: they would be bound to fail. The second was that if leadership move to the bottom, not only do internal relations need to be improved to ensure the market is reached, but new market opportunities also need to be discovered. In order to solve the two issues that Gerstner worried about, Zhang Ruimin realized that Haier also needed to further change from the inverted triangle to a closed-loop networked organization, turning the inverted triangle into a net.

Zhang Ruimin says:

After Haier inverted the organizational triangle, the organizational model was successful in terms of the ZZJYTs, that is, employees were in full contact with users, working together to form a mutual organization. For example, the six refrigerator teams, including R&D, manufacturing, marketing, finance, as well as suppliers and so on, together become a community of interests. The function of second-level ZZJYTs is to provide resources to front-line ZZJYTs. This subversion solved the problems of collaboration among first-level ZZJYTs, but the roles of the original functional departments being turned from supervision to resource providers became more difficult. To deal with these problems, Haier's organizational restructuring took another step forward – turning the inverted triangle into a closed loop network. In this way, the original first-level ZZJYT, second-level ZZJYT and cooperative partners form an LGT, fully collaborative, acting as a platform-based team, with individuals meeting and parting.

For example, looking at Haier's marketing structure in the past, at the top was the national marketing leadership, then there would be managers for marketing to each of the provinces, then one layer for the management of the staff in each city, then another layer of marketing for each county, built up layer upon layer. In a networked organization none of these levels exist, it has become completely flat. Now each county has a team of seven people. They are each responsible for the creation of county-level users, so for example, 300,000 Haier users could be created in a county of 1 million people. These orders would belong to the team, and the team shares the value created by the users.

Thus, Haier has evolved into a platform organization. Many groups can trade on this platform, so they have a parallel relationship. In the past, business processes were connected in a series: first design, then manufacture, then sales, then service. After combining everything though, all relevant personnel participate in every aspect at the same time. For example, when designing, the users and suppliers are involved, and everyone participates in design through the differing platforms. Therefore, in the design phase, it will already have been decided whether the product can be sold on the market.

Haier's innovative ZZJYT model has been confirmed by its results: for three consecutive years, the company has been ranked as the first brand in white goods by the world's most authoritative market research firm, with a turnover in 2011 of ¥150.9 billion globally. From 2007 to 2011, the profit CAGR was 38 per cent, and the cash conversion cycle (CCC) was less than 10 days.

Thirty years of Haier

Transformation of functional departments

In 1992, Haier entered the strategic stage of diversification, moving towards developing freezer and air conditioning businesses. Recently graduated Tan Lixia was assigned to the air conditioning business and competed to take a cashier position.

At that time, China's foreign exchange was under dual control, and each location had a State Administration of Foreign Exchange, responsible for the allocation of foreign exchange. At the same time, companies could also qualify to buy credits on the market. The traders were commonly known as 'red vests', they represented the relevant expertise. Import and export business is an extremely complex financial process, and no one wanted to sign up to learn it, but Tan Lixia took the initiative and applied for this valuable learning opportunity. Although as she said, 'It took us a long time to connect the services.'

The determined effort she made became the starting point

for Tan Lixia's personal development. In 1994, she competed for a position related to the overseas export of air conditioning, and became known for pioneering the demanding requirements of the European market, bringing about a breakthrough. Later, she entered Haier Electronics Import and Export Corporation, just catching the 1995 state-level import tax reform and adjustment period. During three years, Tan Lixia's operational capacity increased rapidly: 'The reason I had so much opportunity to grow despite having just graduated, is really thanks to the Haier platform, unlike many Chinese companies at the time, we were doing things for real, not for show.'

Subsequently, Tan Lixia also worked on the Haier Colour TV export business. In 1999, the Group set up an overseas promotion office, merging the focus of the various export-related businesses. Tan Lixia served as Director of the Integration Division. She used team brainstorming sessions as a way of determining the Haier export process. It would have been very difficult to accomplish this just by relying on individuals. 'What made us feel very proud was that we ordered the entire exportation process. Looking back, the Group did not experience as many problems with its export business as other companies; Haier's export process was very smooth.'

From 2006 onwards, Tan Lixia took over as the Group CFO, and after the integration of financial, human, process, strategy, legal and internal control departments, formed the FU (functional unit) platform, joining with white goods productions and distribution channel integrated services to form the three pillars of the Haier Group. In the Group's networked platform strategy, FU was also actively seeking a breakthrough, transitioning from control to platforms. On the financial side, Tan Lixia was working to create a kind of 'sea, land and air', three-dimensional business model, that is, the financial division grew from standing outside the business, doing the accounting post hoc, to becoming a value creator for the 'sea, land and air' team. 'Land soldiers' refers to the team involved in splitting and thinning the financial accounting functions, creating a one-stop shared service centre. The 'air force' refers to professional financing, for example, foreign exchange, financing, financial management and big data applications. The 'marines' refers to the front-line staff involved in 'front-line combat' with the front-line staff of the micro-enterprises.

Globalization strategy adjustments – cultural integration

Haier established a global strategy to set up Haier factories over-seas, but also made a lot of detours. There is a benchmark for international companies that building a factory outside their home country in order to build a brand will take a minimum of eight years operating at a loss. Haier lost money for almost nine years in the United States.

During the development of the globalization strategy, Zhang Ruimin discovered that before understanding globalization, it was necessary for the brand to be fully localized, and to find locals to do the management. However, despite this, there were many problems. Haier's objective was the localization of the enterprise, but the enterprise was not necessarily competitive, even when fully localized. The globalization of Haier required cross-cultural integration. The question was how to use the culture and the advantages of local people, while at the same time optimizing and enhancing them, so cross-cultural management was a major issue.

On 18 October 2011, Sanyo and Haier Co. signed a merger agreement for the acquisition by Haier of Sanyo's white goods busi-ness in Japan, Vietnam, Indonesia, the Philippines and Malaysia. The head of Japan's largest home appliance chain group, Yamada Denki, later said he did not think that Haier would move so fast: 3,000 channel stores, 33 new Japanese consumer product designs, and 90,000 prototypes were instantly available: 'Haier appliances were doing something unprecedented in the history of Japan.'

With the reform of traditional Japanese corporate culture, cultural integration was achieved, and this was the determining factor of success for future mergers and acquisitions. Japanese enterprises attached great importance to team spirit. The annual awards and lifelong employment systems are fully entrenched. However, in the Internet era, traditional Japanese corporate culture experienced a growing challenge. The system-wide mergers and acquisitions ensured the survival of Sanyo's original excellent corporate culture heritage. At the same time, Haier applied the self-developed management model of individual goals together to the Japanese team. Haier reformed the enterprise while ensuring that they did not violate Japanese law: the original wage system and functional evaluation standards were changed, and market-oriented goals were established to guide the evaluation system; the personnel promotion system generally used by Japanese companies was reformed, and mechanisms which were target and result oriented were established.

Tsutomu Nakagawa is Haier's Sales Director for Japan. According to the Japanese company's traditional performance pay mechanism, market performance and remuneration do not have a close relationship, but after reforming the pay system, he could no longer complete the goals set by his superiors, but instead directly faced his own market, with creating customer value as his mission. Nakagawa, after a period of hesitation, chose to challenge himself, and promised to double his goals. Another manager, due to the success of the planned programme of market competitiveness achieving excess profits for the enterprise, was promoted to Planning Division Head at the age of only 35. This was unthinkable at traditional Sanyo.

Zhang Ruimin summed up the Sanyo merger:

The Japanese brand of professionalism, combined with our 'individuals coming together' model of management, created a threefold increase in our half-year results. This success story also allows us to see another role for the localization of companies, which is to maximize the integration of local human resources. Haier's individual goals together with its win-win philosophy and cultural identity along with mature corporate culture guarantees successful complex mergers and acquisitions, and reaches synergies in the shortest time possible.

On 11 September 2012, Haier spent about $766 million to procure an 80 per cent stake in Fisher & Paykel, later wholly owning New Zealand's largest home appliance maker. Fisher & Paykel's brand positioning was as a luxury appliance firm, but its problem was its lack of global penetration. Haier had a lack of high-end brands, but strong experience in global development; it was these complementary advantages that contributed to the success of the acquisition.

Haier completed two major acquisitions in two years showing Haier's adjustments in globalization strategy, from freely opening foreign markets towards directly acquiring foreign brands. This is the change in Haier's process of globalization from 'going out' to 'coming in', and then gradually to the 'growing upwards' stage.

On 6 June 2016, Qingdao Haier, a Shanghai stock exchange listed company that is 41 per cent owned by Haier Group, confirmed acquisition of GE Appliances from General Electric. It marks the beginning of GE Appliances being part of Qingdao Haier and is another milestone in Haier's globalization.

Chinese appliance makers currently account for 50 per cent of the world's total. That is, half of all global home appliances are produced in China. However, independent Chinese branded appliances only hold about 3 per cent of overseas markets, and of that 3 per cent, 80 per cent comes from Haier. If people see a Chinese home appliance brand overseas, there is a 90 per cent chance that it is Haier. This is the greatest affirmation of the Haier brand overseas.

Thirty years of Haier

Wang Yingmin – Individual goals together stimulate the entrepreneurship of Japanese employees

Haier Asia International employee Wang Yingmin says of working in Japan: 'Now in Japan, locals know Haier, and they are willing to talk more about us. More and more young people in Japan recognize Haier's culture, and are willing to join the team. This was unthinkable in the past.'

In 2007 at the end of nearly 10 years of human resources work, Wang Yingmin, who is of Japanese origin, volunteered to go to Haier Asia International, with the idea of 'taking the culture of Haier to the Japanese workers'. He worked there for seven years.

After the acquisition of Sanyo white goods, Haier gradually grew Japan. The group simultaneously operated two brands in the local area – Haier and AQUA; in shopping malls in Japan, Haier is the only Chinese brand standing shoulder to shoulder with Japanese brands. Haier culture rapidly affected Japanese workers.

'When the Japanese team had just joined Haier, they went on a business trip to Qingdao to cooperate with the Qingdao R&D team, regularly visiting to get technical guidance. Do not even ask what kind of effect this had. They thought they had to learn the technical aspect of the products, but that the relationship between how to develop products on the market and how well they would sell them was not their problem. They no longer think this.'

Wang Yingmin says that their team included a multi-door refrigerators team head, Yamaguchi, who had been involved in the R&D of appliances, and had been a senior figure in the Sanyo organization for some years. But there was simply no way that Sanyo would let him serve as the head of a project.

'In Japanese companies, staff struggle through at least 40 or 50 years before being able to lead a project, but in Haier's individual goals together model, Yamaguchi was able to become the leader of a project. Now he regularly works in Huangdao (an area of Qingdao where many Haier factories are located) and immediately resolves any problems that arise. He is the owner of his projects and is completely self-driven.'

At Haier Asia International, the income of employees is linked with their target market and their effect on the market. When making changes, Wang Yingmin thinks that one of the most important things about cross-cultural integration is to respect people:

> The Japanese work ethic and teamwork is very strong, and once they recognize your culture, corporate loyalty will be very high. Haier's individual goals together, 'high orders, high reward' enterprise culture is totally different to the seniority systems applied at Japanese companies, so at the beginning the Japanese employees did not believe in it, but after some personal experience, they began to think that this model is more conducive to creating value.

There were two reasons for the early success with Japanese companies. First, teamwork, and second a wage-seniority system. In the era of large-scale manufacturing, these two factors meant that 'Made in Japan' was another way of saying high quality at low cost. But in the mass customization era, enterprises have to meet the individual needs of users. The wage-seniority system is an inherent part of Japanese corporate culture, and the biggest problem is that the employees listen to the leadership instead of listening to users. Under this system, the creativity of staff is not given free rein, and the space for promotion is very limited. After Haier's acquisition of Sanyo white goods, the promotion system was changed, and a mechanism by which people are paid for orders was established.

In Wang Yingmin's opinion, Haier's stimulation of employee creativity is very important: 'Over the years, Haier has been in the business of people.' His own experience is the best proof of this. During his 30 years at Haier, Wang Yingmin worked in Supply and Marketing, Human Resources, and the Haier Asia Office. 'Haier has never said anything about seniority, so when I was appointed Head of Supply, there were people older than me and with more qualifications than me.'

Thinking back to his 30-year journey with Haier, Wang Yingmin feels fulfilled: 'During my youth I spent all my time at Haier, so I am very lucky; it was a worthy use of my time. Now, most of my work is in Japan, where every year the annual Spring Festival Gala is organized by the Chinese Embassy and Haier is sitting in the front. Next to us there are some state-owned banks, airlines and the like.' Wang Yingmin is full of the pride which longer-term employees often express about Haier.

Thirty years of Haier

Diao Yunfeng – From promotion of brand globalization to the creation of a global platform

In 2014 Diao Yunfeng celebrated his nineteenth year at Haier. This makes the Group Vice President and International Trading Company General Manager a long-standing employee.

In his 19 years at Haier, Diao Yunfeng has experienced the company's three stages of development: the diversification strategy, the internationalization strategy and the global brand strategy. He has seen China's local brand grow to become the first ranked white goods brand in the world. In those 19 years, Diao Yunfeng has always dealt with overseas markets, as he says, 'Even my dreams happen overseas.'

Diao Yunfeng says that by far the most memorable point in his career was the year Haier entered the US market. In the US in the 1990s, five mainstream local brands accounted for about 95 per cent of market share. Korean brands had attempted to seize the market using the low-cost route. After a running series of research projects, Haier executives decided to adopt a gap strategy, digging into local user requirements to pry open the market.

As a result, Diao Yunfeng found local teams to conduct research on user needs. Diao Yunfeng says they found something interesting while doing wine cooler research. The US market offered many large wine coolers, which only high-end consumers could afford, but many middle-class families also have wine storage needs, and yet there were no companies involved in this market. In response to this need, Haier developed a wine cooler aimed at the American middle-class market. The wine cooler was noiseless, with a transparent glass door, so it could be treated almost like a work of art in the kitchen.

'At first, we found the person responsible at the headquarters of a local distributor, and we discussed sales matters with them, but we were rejected,' Diao Yunfeng recalls. At that time foreign companies we often added into sales channels but quickly withdrew from the market due to poor management, therefore, this channel was sceptical about the new brand. So Haier adjusted its tactics, first selecting a store from the distributions network, and then making a deal with the store. It was agreed that the market would be tested in the store, and if the wine cooler sold well, the store would purchase the goods. If sales were poor, Haier would withdraw the wine coolers from sale. The goods sold out in just a few short days. 'A few days later, the head of this store contacted us proactively and asked if he could continue to sell our wine coolers.' Currently, Haier brand products are stationed in the top ten mainstream sales channels in the United States.

Despite his 19 years in the company, Diao Yunfeng felt like a newcomer when entering the Internet era, and embarking on a journey of innovation and entrepreneurship that was different to previous brand building efforts he had been involved in.

At that time, the Internet was starting to allow buyers and sellers from around the world to come together, so many small and medium companies involved in foreign trade were born in China, but they faced many difficulties due to limitations of scale in foreign trade. Haier opened up the overseas markets many years ago, so the company has accumulated a wealth of channels, logistics and other resources. Diao Yunfeng says that Haier's opening not only allowed foreign resources to enter the Haier platform, it also involved using Haier resources to help the Internet platforms provide more win-win opportunities for partners.

The result of this thinking was the creation of a transnational e-commerce platform. Diao Yunfeng says that at that time, China's small and medium enterprises were mainly working on the production of single products. For example, if they were making machines for bean curd, then all they did was make those products. Diao Yunfeng's team took these scattered products and tidied them into different programs. At the same time, they also provided full-process service from ordering to design, quality control, storage and logistics. Diao Yunfeng says that their goal was to ensure that trading opportunities could all be connected, so people who did not understand trading could easily enter the market.

Talking about his new role, Diao Yunfeng becomes emotional when he says that he moved from being an 'implementer' to a 'connector'. 'Previously we were working on a corporate brand, now we are making platforms for e-commerce, the challenges of which can be easily imagined.' But, Diao Yunfeng and his team believe that as long as they find the right road, they don't need to worry about its length.

The world is your R&D department

Zhang Ruimin believes that innovation capacity is related to the degree to which resources can be integrated. 'Wikinomics argues that the world is your R&D department.'

Thus, R&D should be an open platform. In the past, companies tended to treat research and development as a very confidential department, but if the research and development is moved onto an open platform, there is an unexpected amplification of resources. Procter & Gamble's former Chief Operating Officer discussed this with Zhang Ruimin. P&G's product range is very large, and very consistent with the needs of users. A very important factor in enabling this was the development of an open platform. P&G has 9,000 internal R&D personnel, but this 9,000 become more than 1.8 million developers by means of open social platform integration.

The open platform not only brings together researchers, it can also bring users together. Haier Crystal Washing Machines are billed as the world's quietest washing machines, and users determined its R&D direction. Research and development personnel can interact with 2 million users through the Internet, acquiring a large amount of data on user needs. Because they are autonomous and self-financing, R&D bodies first forecast the value of meeting the needs of the user, then worldwide, world-class technology and equipment resources are integrated. This led to the creation of a very quiet washing machine with excellent washing results. After putting the product on the market, it rapidly drove Haier's washing machine market share to the number one position, four times the average growth rate in the industry.

Zhang Ruimin says:

In the past, we spent lots of money digging for personnel, but now, as long as they agree with the Haier culture, the design team can be independent, and we establish contractual relationships with them. We do not develop products, instead we develop the market by capturing users. I just set what kind of user groups I want to capture, and what kind of reward we could achieve if we developed that market, and then the actual design is a totally independent decision.

Now, Haier owns five global R&D centres (China, Asia, the Americas, Europe and Australia). These centres are platform-based R&D centres forming the open system in which the world is Haier's R&D department. Each Haier R&D centre can operate independently, but they can also coordinate when needed. According to the local technical advantages, the R&D centres have different specialisms. For example, North America's scientific and technological innovation advantages are prominent, so Haier put their forward-looking R&D and creative platform in North America. Europe has obvious advantages in technology transfer and incubation of products, and industrial design, so Haier put its core technology research and technical feasibility analysis in Europe. The Japanese centre is focused on fine management and control advantages; and the office in China is focused on the industrialization of products.

These five independently operating R&D centres with their synergies comprise Haier's open global R&D system, with an industry-leading speed of innovation. This is what creates global user resources. Haier's innovative French and Italian refrigerators have not only won the acceptance of global users, but have become something that others in the industry are attempting to imitate.

6

Networked Haier (2012–present)

Moments of shock – the fall of giants

Traditional industry has been deeply impacted by the digital economy ever since it arrived.

After General Motors filed for bankruptcy protection in June 2009, the threat of bankruptcy began to hover around the manufacturing sector like a ghost. The American motor city of Detroit has been on the verge of bankruptcy ever since. Ford simply said that they are not a manufacturing company, but a technology company, thereby redrawing the boundaries of traditional industry.

However, some elements of the auto industry saw new life in an area totally unrelated to manufacturing. Tesla, a technology company making electric cars using IT technology was becoming exceedingly popular.

In January 2012, 100-year-old Kodak filed for bankruptcy protection. This giant had almost ruled the film industry, and had always been at the forefront of technology. Kodak developed the first digital camera, but failed to recognize the power of numbers. Eventually, Kodak was defeated by the rise of Japanese digital camera manufacturers.

In 2013, another industry giant almost fell. Nokia, a Finnish mobile phone manufacturer, was the standing global handset market share champion for 16 years; no one could have anticipated that what would almost defeat it would be the 2007 launch of the iPhone. Apple and Google redefined the mobile phone, giving Nokia a final wake-up call, but they had already lost the opportunity to mount a comeback. Finally, the former giant had to cut off its arm to survive, and sold the mobile phone business to Microsoft. On the other hand, Microsoft targeted the mobile Internet market but failed to dominate the field.

Another former star of the mobile phone industry was also beaten by its arrogance. BlackBerry completely ignored the demands of the market; they stubbornly persisted in their beliefs that safety was the core requirement for mobile phones, and that the full keyboard was a good response to user interface requirements. BlackBerry's prospects are uncertain, but one thing is for sure: they have lost the ability to compete in existing markets.

Hewlett-Packard too broke under the pressure of the market. After its 2001 acquisition of Compaq, HP had overtaken Dell to claim the top spot in the PC industry, becoming the world's largest IT company. But too many products and services were being provided by HP. The company was unable to focus on any one area. HP's printers, servers, PCs, storage and network devices faced cheap commodity pricing, service homogeneity, and very thin profits.

Dell's direct sales model had been brilliant as it eliminated middlemen. Direct sales had also helped them to build closer relationships with customers and create greater value. However, the development of the Internet meant that Dell's unique direct marketing advantages were no longer so unique. A lack of R&D and innovative capabilities added to their difficulties.

The former giants thought that they represented the direction of the industry, but they ignored the buds of disruptive innovation. The success of many innovative start-up companies has been built amid the ruins of former giants. This is why Bill Gates has said, 'Microsoft is always only 18 months away from bankruptcy,' and why Pony Ma says that when the giant has fallen, its body is still warm.

The big data era

Big data is the inevitable outcome of bringing the information society into the Internet era. Each user creates large amounts of detailed data simply by using a smartphone. The volume of data is not only massive, but it is real-time and dynamic. After the data is effectively mined and analysed, it will undoubtedly become an important basis for decision-making and governance.

In *Big Data: A Revolution That Will Transform How We Live, Work, and Think*, Viktor Mayer-Schönberger and Kenneth Cukier suggest that most companies are still in the era of using big data as a marketing tool. However, big data has the potential to help companies change their business and profit models.

The United States and Britain may have been the first two countries to be aware of big data. The Obama administration included big data in the country's national strategy, and the British government proposed the concept of 'data rights'. Britain and America have each built their own open governments, and they have also called on other national governments to transform and adapt to the new era.

Cloud computing

Cloud computing is a new Internet-based IT service, use and delivery model; it usually involves providing dynamically scalable and often virtual resources via the Internet. Users no longer need to know the details of the infrastructure when using a cloud service, they do not necessarily need to have much expertise, and they do not have direct control over it. In the Software as a Service (SaaS) model, users can access software and data services. Service providers maintain the infrastructure and service platform in order to maintain normal operations. SaaS is often referred to as 'on demand software', and it is usually charged according to the volume utilized, although sometimes it is offered on a subscription basis.

SaaS allows companies to borrow outsourced hardware,

software, maintenance and support services from the service provider to reduce IT operating costs. In addition, since the applications are provided together, updates can be published in real time, without the user having to manually update or install new software. The drawback of SaaS is that the user's data is stored on the service provider's server, introducing some risks around the privacy and security of the information.

Users access cloud services via a browser, desktop application or mobile application so the enterprise is able to rapidly deploy applications, and reduce the complexity of management and maintenance costs, allowing IT resources to be quickly reallocated to cope with rapidly changing business needs.

Cloud computing depends on the sharing of resources to achieve economies of scale, just like other infrastructure (such as the power grid). Service providers integrate a large number of resources for multiple users, so users can easily request (rent) more resources, and adjust the amount they use at any time, releasing any unwanted resources back to the other users. Thus, the user does not need to purchase a lot of resources to meet short-term peak demand; access to cloud based resources can simply be adjusted according to need. Service providers can rent unused resources to other users, even adjusting the rent in accordance with overall demand.

Regardless of whether a company uses a private, public or hybrid cloud the cloud has opened the road to 'smart manufacturing'. Most traditional manufacturing industries deploy the cloud through applications such as desktop clouds and cloud finance, as well as ERP, and OA system applications. This can improve management efficiency. At the same time, cloud computing is the basis for the broader implementation of big data. Big data is the key to future applications for both manufacturing and services.

Cloud computing offers the opportunity for companies to use Internet-based cloud computing services instead of expensive physical servers.

Of course, the physical server providers will not just wait around to become extinct but will find ways to cope with the changes. In May 2014, the IBM SaaS 100+ team sent a letter to Zhang Ruimin to encourage Haier to accelerate the process of embracing the mobile Internet. Saas 100+ offered a cloud-based computing system encompassing 100 IBM applications and services, one of which was big data analysis technology. The IBM team even wrote movingly at the end of the letter: 'Twenty-nine years ago, you broke the door to the outside world for Haier with a hammer, and today we look forward to working with Smart Haier to walk into every user's heart.'

Internet of things

The IOT (Internet of Things) is the system in which an Internet-based, traditional telecommunications network or other information carrier is utilized, so that all ordinary physical objects can be independently accessed. In the IOT, everyone can use electronic tags to link a real object to the Internet, and their specific position can be found on the Internet. Through the IOT, a central computer can be used for machine, device and staff centralization, and management and control; household equipment and cars can also be controlled remotely, while real-time location and anti-theft and other applications are also enabled.

In the consumer electronics industry, the initial skirmishes have begun as the IOT is applied in the smart home market. In June 2014, at the WWDC 2014 forum, Apple launched the brand new HomeKit smart home platform, which can integrate a variety of smart home apps, so that by pressing a button on your iPhone, you can remotely activate lighting, door locks and temperature controls. Using Siri, this can be voice-activated, while security monitoring functions are also facilitated.

Among the first batch of appliance manufacturers to access HomeKit, together with familiar names such as Philips and Honeywell, was Haier, the only Chinese manufacturer. In other words, Haier is the world's only official Apple MFi certified white goods brand, and the company's Tianzun Air Conditioner also became a member of the certified household electrical appliance family. Before Apple released the HomeKit on 17 March, Haier had released a new U+ smart life operating system. It only takes this system 12 seconds to bring about interoperability among all smart home terminals and it is compatible with Apple and other brands.

On 28 July 2013, Haier launched a new corporate logo and slogan. This is the Haier brand image it adopted after network strategy. The new company slogan, 'your smart life, my smart life', reflects the era of the Internet, the relationship between people, the relationship between Haier and users, and the fact that inter-activity is everywhere, while also implying Haier's ambitions in the area of smart appliances.

Smart home applications can include audio and video resources, personal multimedia, information services and appli-ance networking. Although the promotion of smart homes is still in its infancy, representing a minority of business and home applications, market research firm IDC predicts that the value of the smart home market will grow significantly, and expects it to reach $51.77 billion by 2020. The biggest challenge for the future is how to achieve a global industry-standard for all applications.

The BAT fight

BAT is a combination of the first English letters of the big three Internet companies in China: Baidu, Alibaba and Tencent. The BAT members lead the Chinese Internet, but there is fierce com-petition between the three and IT news headlines in China in recent years have most often related to one of them. The competi-tion among the three ranges across business areas from instant messaging to online financial products, from electronic business platforms to local services.

In addition to the products each has introduced, acquisitions are their primary means of doing battle. Someone said that for non-BAT domestic Internet companies, there are two possible outcomes: separately going onto the market or being acquired by one of the BAT club members.

On 19 September 2014, BAT member Alibaba was listed on the NYSE, with an issue price of $68, an opening price of $92.70, and a first daily closing price of $93.89, representing a market capitalization of over $230 billion. Alibaba became the Internet company with the world's second largest market capitalization, second only to Google; they also became the company with the third largest market capitalization in China after China Mobile and PetroChina. On 28 October 2014, the share price hit a new record of $100.5, meaning that the market capitalization reached $247 billion, making it larger than Wal-Mart, the world's largest retailer in terms of revenue.

Alibaba's IPO financing reached $21.77 billion, making it the largest IPO in the history of US stocks. These results meant that Alibaba surpassed eBay and Amazon as the world's number one electronic business platform. Its retail businesses (Taobao, Tmall, Juhuasuan) have 279 million active consumers, 8.5 million active sellers, and 188 million monthly active mobile phone users, with an annual trading volume of ¥1.5 trillion (about twice that of Amazon), and mobile transactions amounting to $232 billion. Taobao has more than 100 million unique visitors every single day, while Alipay has 300 million active users.

China's protection policies have been helpful to Alibaba, Baidu, Tencent, Xiaomi and other Chinese Internet companies, but these companies are committed to meeting market demand, developing core technology and constructing their own ecosystems through acquisitions or strategic partnerships, while expanding their mobile applications and O2O (Online to Offline) business territory. At the same time, they have also developed their own unique innovations.

Yahoo's former global vice president, Zhang Chen, believes that China's Internet is entering a period of rapid development. In the mobile Internet field, Chinese Internet companies in many ways have exceeded their North American peers. Although early on, the mode of operation was often called C2C (Copy to China), this situation has gradually changed, especially in the mobile Internet field. Chinese Internet companies have come from behind to catch-up with their peers.

In Zhang Chen's opinion, the reason for this phenomenon is the rise of mobile Internet, and more importantly, economic innovation, meaning innovation in terms of the product, production, markets and business models, resource allocation and organizational structure. Taxi software, mobile commerce, mobile games and other existing innovative platforms are popular throughout China; there has also been an integration of the Internet for finance, manufacturing and other traditional industries.

The Xiaomi phenomenon

The meteoric rise of Xiaomi, has taken it from nothing to become a phenomenal product. Xiaomi phone fever has resulted in a very loyal fan base, and word of mouth recommendations continue to expand the company's market influence.

Tens of millions of users became Xiaomi's research and development assistance group, providing huge volumes of demands, comments and suggestions. Xiaomi interacts with its users through micro-blogging on Weibo, WeChat and forums, and depending on demand, the Xiaomi phone system is updated every week. With each update a few dozen or more functions are added, one third of which are directly suggested by users.

More importantly, Xiaomi has a fully asset-light model, unlike traditional mobile phone manufacturers. There are no sales channels, and they do not own their own factories. Xiaomi has used Internet technology to successfully transform the mobile phone industry. Its Dell-style model of supply chain management brings about zero inventory, with supply on demand; its Amazon-like channel pattern reduces distribution costs; and its use of social media results in zero cost marketing.

Xiaomi phones have only been established for a few years, but their turnover has already reached ¥30 billion, so the company valuation is as high as $10 billion. Almost overnight Xiaomi became the heroes of the Internet, subverting traditional industries, and in China, created a new concept, 'Internet Thinking'.

The habits of a lot of Chinese were changing without our realizing it: watching *House of Cards* on the computer accustomed us to online video, and using WeChat to split bills accustomed us to mobile payments. Now, before we walk into a restaurant, we check public feedback apps and when we are driving, we rely on satellite navigation apps.

We are all Internet users, and we are also still users of traditional products such as refrigerators, washing machines, televisions, and so on. Traditional products must adopt Internet thinking. For manufacturers, the question of how to transform seems imminent.

The Chinese economy's 'new normal'

The Decision on Major Issues Concerning Comprehensively Deepening Reforms was adopted at the close of the Third Plenary Session of the Eighteenth CPC Central Committee on 12 November 2013. The reform of the economic system was focused on efforts to deepen the all-round reform. The core aim was to deal with the relationship between government and the market, making the market play a decisive role in the allocation of resources and allowing government to play a suitable role.

The decision stated that diversified ownership integrated by state capital, collective capital and private capital would be the prime method for materializing the basic economic system (i.e. socialist market economy), helping improve functions, increase value and promote the competitiveness of state capital. More SOEs and other ownership enterprises were to be allowed to develop into mixed-ownership enterprises and non-state shares were to be allowed in state capital investment projects.

Through the main realization of transforming the shareholding system to a public ownership system, to acknowledging the fact that the mixed economic system is key to the basic economy, the integration of state-owned and private enterprises became the highlight of a new round of SOE reform. Xinhua Net called this the 'Advancement of Nationals Together'.

In May 2014, 'new normal' first appeared in statements made by General Secretary Xi Jinping when visiting Henan. Xi pointed out that, 'China is still in a significant period of strategic opportunity. We must boost our confidence, adapt to the new normal condition based on the characteristics of China's economic growth in the current phase and stay cool-minded. In terms of tactics, we should attach great importance to the prevention of risks, with early planning, so that come a rainy day, we can make timely response measures, so as to minimize the negative effects.' On 29 July, during a seminar with non-Party members, Xi Jinping again suggested that it was necessary to recognize the characteristics of China's stage of development, further boost confidence and adapt to the new normal.

Publicly reinforcing these ideas, *The People's Daily* published a series of comments which analysed China's economic situation from multiple perspectives and provided a specific interpretation of the content and meaning of the Chinese economy's 'new normal'.

The *People's Daily* stated: 'The new normal is a new exploration, to reform towards openness, and to give full play to the decisive role of the market, stimulating business and social vitality, cultivating the endogenous force for driving economic development, and accelerating economic transformation and upgrading structural optimization, so as to improve people's livelihoods.'

Network Strategy – things are the opposite of people

On 26 December 2012, Zhang Ruimin announced that Haier had entered the fifth stage of its strategic development – the Network Strategy stage.

The Network Strategy includes two parts, network marketing and network business.

Network marketing first refers to the user network. In the past there has always been some kind of contract governing the relationship between customers and businesses. This contract may be direct or it may be implied. What companies are not used to is that there is now also an agreement between users and this is the way they act together or treat each other. Such agreements are very important in the social context, and in some cases, more important than the agreement between businesses and customers. People can now easily arrange all kinds of groups, activities and commercial forces on the Internet and this has shaken many enterprises and the fundamentals of the way they do business, even destroying some of them.

The marketing system is also networked, becoming both decentralized and cooperative. For example, all the online shops are dispersed, forming a shop network, which is extremely decentralized, but at the same time remains highly cooperative. This is completely different from the traditional large shopping malls. It leads to lean manufacturing and precision marketing. Online shopping price is very low, may be thirty or fifty per cent cheaper than that of a physical store, but the delivery can be accurate and efficient, completely subverting the traditional model.

Zhang Ruimin says of these changes: 'The same thing, but different people.' The things are still the original products, but the people are not the original people. External users, and also internal employees have changed, but both are driving the business. Externally, users drive the business. Internally, staff drive the business.

Zhang Ruimin suggests that the future form of business organization will be 'dispersed cooperative'; the existing form of management we are familiar with is coming to an end. Traditional economic management theory is based on Adam Smith's ideas, which led to the development of scientific management and a hierarchical division of labour. Even today, enterprises rely on production being a line process and the organization a pyramid. However, these are both completely inappropriate for the Internet age as outside the enterprise users have become a network, and have joint capacity for action; accordingly, within the enterprise, employees must direct the business in order to accurately grasp the trend towards fragmentation and the user's needs for personalization.

Zhang Ruimin summarizes the characteristics of networked business as borderless, leaderless and scale-free:

1. Business has no borders, so Haier must change to becoming a connected ecosystem with ZZJYTs as the individual cells, and full of teams with a goals-oriented recruitment and dismissal platform.

2. Management has no leaders. Haier is exploring the use of autonomous micro-enterprises, in which each employee becomes a micro-company in and of themselves and the users are the real leaders.

3. The supply chain is scale-free, as this is a complex network of critical nodes. Each critical node has autonomy and vitality, and can serve niche and mass users at the same time.

This strategic direction was announced at the Golden Hammer Awards ceremony symbolizing the spirit of Haier's entrepreneurship and innovation. After the business process re-engineering, Haier began yet another unprecedented process of change, and the significance and scope of this is far beyond that of previous changes.

It really is a huge subversion, even terms like 'inside / outside', 'up / down' and other binary concepts lose their meaning. In the networked world, boundaries are no longer clear, everything comes back to the core of the business, and how this core is implemented in the business environment where user needs are the dominant force for change.

The Golden Hammer Award.

Zhang Ruimin at the Golden Hammer Awards

Zhang Ruimin – Leading enterprises and leading business models

We have now reached our current Network Strategy stage, although we are continuing to explore the Internet age. We are using a concept rooted in Chinese philosophy, 'thinking that we have no value', meaning that we need to overcome the idea that we have succeeded, so that we continually focus on overcoming our weaknesses. Winning today is not sufficient, as we also need to win tomorrow. We need to strive for sustainable innovation, quickly growing a series of competitive advantages and then upgrading, seizing fleeting or instantaneous opportunities.

We had to determine a strategy for the Internet age. Our goal was to create the best user experience possible. In *The Third Industrial Revolution* Jeremy Rifkin said that the third industrial revolution has a scattered, cooperative nature and a flat structure based on community gathering, and he proposed that we move from 'globalization' to 'intercontinentalization'. Now we are moving back to 'globalization', back from 'intercontinentalization', even back to 'nationalization'. But this is not a backward step, it is a response to individualized needs. The Internet age has changed the problem of information asymmetry which was found in the traditional economy in which users knew less than businesses, information was in the hands of businesses, and the business could give the user what the business wanted to provide. In the past the business winners were the biggest advertisers, now, users can get all the information they want on the Internet, so businesses have become passive. Enterprises have to listen to the users. This is equivalent to the users becoming leaders of the enterprises.

Intercontinentalization may further transform to become regionalization, because of the flat structure created by community gathering. American industry has actually begun to do this – some companies have already begun reshoring.

American firm GE returned its production base for washing machines and water heaters from Suzhou back to Louisville. The company's Union President spoke to the US media, saying that they moved back home to manufacture products in the United States, where manufacturing costs were 20–30 per cent lower than in China, thanks to their intelligent manufacturing. In addition, they can create value based on the needs of their users.

In the dozen or so years since Haier set up a factory in South Carolina, China's manufacturing advantage has indeed declined. If Chinese companies are not innovative, still primarily serving as OEMs, soon there will be no foothold. When we started production in 2001, South Carolina had some of the lowest wages in the US. The salary offered by Haier was certainly not the lowest in the country, but even so the wages of American workers were nineteen times the wages of Chinese workers. By 2013, the differential had reduced, so American workers were making only four times the wages of a Chinese worker. In the US oil costs less than half the amount it costs in China. We compared the shipments collected from South Carolina and delivered to New Jersey, with those from Qingdao to Shanghai, which is about the same distance. The road transport costs in China were eighteen times greater than those in the US, mainly because of the cost of Chinese road tolls.

What should Chinese enterprises do? Central government has advocated upgrading; I believe we should accelerate this process. Speed is primarily produced by innovation; without innovation it would be difficult to make any upgrades.

I think enterprises fall into two types: one I call leading enterprises and one I call treadmill enterprises. The treadmill enterprises term is my own; the leading enterprises concept was from ideas about disruptive innovation and continuity put forward by Clayton M. Christensen. Disruptive innovation means completely changing the existing system to lead the industry – Apple is an example of this kind of innovator. Sustaining innovation is the basis of continuous improvement. It requires a lot of effort, but this may not necessarily bring about good results. An example was the attempts to find methods to continue extracting oil from depleted oil fields. The US shale gas innovation took a different approach and has solved the problem, opening an alternative to oil fields. As a result, American gas prices are very low now, and the reserves are huge, so they can even export large quantities.

If a business is not a leading enterprise, then it is just a treadmill enterprise. They run very fast on the treadmill, and put in lots of mileage, but they are only staying on the spot. Many companies are like this, it is the cause of price competition and homogenization of competition, when everyone is very busy and works very hard, but in the end, the company makes no profit. Chinese enterprises should become leading enterprises, not just treadmill enterprises.

Thirty years of Haier

Zhou Yunjie – Subversion is achieving success by denying yourself

In 1988, Haier received its first batch of college students, more than 70, including Haier's current rotating presidents Zhou Yunjie and Liang Haishan.

This was during Haier's brand strategy stage. Because domestic demand amplified, there was a rapid rise in the number of domestic appliance manufacturers, and a wave of panic buying, so a price surge occurred. Haier refused to participate in this, instead, focusing their efforts on quality. This approach puzzled the young team members at Haier; Zhou Yunjie clearly remembers that, at that time, Zhang Ruimin gave the following explanation: when building a skyscraper you need bigger foundations than you do if you are building a house. Do not worry, because what we are doing is creating a world-class brand.

Zhou Yunjie understood the truth of this long-term strategy. He started at the grassroots, at refrigerator factory sales level, moving from salesperson to deputy director, and then director of the Second Refrigerator Plant. In 1995, as Haier was merging and expanding, Zhou Yunjie was in charge of the refrigerator business; he served as general manager of the listed company. In 1999, Haier underwent its process re-engineering, and Zhou Yunjie became the probationary group vice president, in charge of market integration. Haier underwent a golden period of rapid growth during this period.

Quickly, Zhou Yunjie felt the growing pains. During the process of re-engineering, Haier began to attempt platformization, creating purchasing, marketing and other major resource platforms. For a manufacturing enterprise used to linear resource management, this was something almost unimaginable. 'At that time, I felt that the research into refrigerator products was already hard enough. All of a sudden many products were integrated onto a single platform, this was totally unthinkable.' Zhou Yunjie said that it felt like changing the engine of an aeroplane mid-flight.

Zhou Yunjie was responsible for commercial development from September 1999 until May 2000. At that time the information systems were still inadequate, so at the end of the day, after sales data was integrated, at around 9 p.m., a global conference call was made, and it would not finish until after midnight. 'This situation was very painful, because a lot of things were broken, and nothing new was set up. The risk was huge.' Zhou Yunjie's pain was in stark contrast to the comfort the organizational change was designed to create, and was made worse because there had been a decline in Haier's performance.

Once, Zhang Ruimin participated in a conference call

being hosted by Zhou Yunjie, 'I was very stressed, as I could not achieve the targets. But CEO Zhang said it did not matter, there were problems. He said that the key was to use the daily clearing process to see whether the problem and potential solutions could be found.' Even up to the present day, Zhang Ruimin still has the same requirements of workers: you cannot hide problems, but must take the initiative to find a solution to them. The most important thing is to have the correct direction.

Recently, Haier has begun the more difficult transition to the Internet. Zhou Yunjie is now an Industry Head, in Haier's terms, in charge of distribution services, and for him this brings significant challenges, since the industry head is the most critical node for this closed-loop transformation. The degree of enthusiasm of the industry head and the subversion of the process will directly determine the success or failure of Haier's transformation. Zhou Yunjie once again has to change the plane's engine mid-flight.

The out-of-control organization

In 2013, Zhang Ruimin, set out a clear strategic Internet framework at the Haier Annual Innovation Conference: business without borders, management without leadership, supply chain which is scale-free. This was a very radical strategic framework as far as the outside world could see, because every single point represented a war with the standard ideology found in management textbooks. Everyone claims that the Internet can subvert the traditional, but for many people, this is just lip service – especially for entrepreneurs as no one talks about subverting themselves. It is not because they are weak or short-sighted, but because the magnitude of the subversion is too large, making control extremely difficult.

But, Zhang Ruimin has reversed this thinking. He thinks that the networked organization should go out of control, only then can his Internet framework be achieved. If Haier can achieve self-organization, the final result of the transformation will be that Haier will move from being a traditional linear manufacturing company, to a continually growing platform based on Internet nodes, where users are part of every stage of the production process, and even the decision about what should be produced is determined by the user. This requires an open platform with excellent awareness and the ability to work in an open fashion; in other words, Haier will no longer be Haier. Zhang Ruimin wants to remove the Haier from Haier, stripping out all the elements of the company's previous success.

Since 2013, Haier has entered its Network Strategy development stage. This deep organizational change and operation mechanism is fully focused around the goal of creating the best user experience. It does this by actively exploring networked resources, networked organization and networked users to create a business ecosystem using shared stakeholders. On the operational level, interaction with the users is enabled through the Haier official website (www.haier.com), Haier user community (bbs.haier.com), the Casarte official website (www.casarte.cn), Haier Mall (www.ehaier.com), www.hijike.com and external resources. This allows real-time understanding of user needs. Through the R&D resources platform (hope.haier.com), resource cloud platform (v.ihaier.com), Haier innovation platform (www.ihaier.com) and other resources, the dynamic introduction of world-class R&D, design, supply chain and other resources is facilitated. This allows Haier to provide the best resources and support experience to users. Precision marketing operations have been facilitated by building big data platforms and exploring interactive marketing models; supply chain modulation and intelligent manufacturing have been promoted allowing accurate and efficient customization; micro-enterprise operating mechanisms have been introduced, stimulating the entrepreneurial energy of employees, transforming and upgrading the entire enterprise.

Starting from the second half of 2013, Haier promoted the new idea of 'registered staff' and 'online staff'. Zhang Ruimin hoped that through the network structure, organizational boundaries could be moved closer to the user by means of the Internet. Resources outside the organization have been completely opened up. What is more, employees can become true 'entrepreneurs', allowing them to find their own entrepreneurial opportunities on the large platform provided by Haier. At the same time, employees are able to make use of the internal venture capital mechanisms, and can also go outside of Haier to mobilize resources before establishing their own micro-enterprises.

The number of Haier employees had grown to 80,000, but now this thinking has been reversed. Numbers have been reduced to 50,000, and will eventually reach the ideal state where there are only a few staff, and the work is done through outsourcing, collaboration and partnerships. Haier has completely removed the concepts of 'inside' and 'outside' from the organization, replacing these ideas with the concepts of 'registered' and 'online'. The only word to describe this transformation is 'revolutionary'.

Zhang Ruimin – Online and registered

We refer to staff as being online or registered. We may have many online staff, but fewer registered staff.

I hope that staff can turn into interfaces, and that these interfaces will access large teams of people, but these teams are online, not registered. Online teams can always be changed. If we made a movie for example, we would require a producer, a film crew and actors, all of whom would be recruited on a temporary basis, only until the film is finished. If we wanted to make another movie the team could come together again, or, depending on the views of the investors we may hire a different team, or a big name actor. Only two or three production staff would need to be permanently employed to bring in investment, plan production and assemble the film crew. Members temporarily joining together and parting uses the same idea. There are problems to resolve, but this is the direction in which we wish to move. We want to create a structure that is completely different to our original business model.

We used to use the IBM Cultivation System to select people, train them, use and then retain them. The process was very complicated. However, it is not suitable for the age of the Internet, where our personnel management uses the wiki concept, harnessing external talents rather than limited to our own human resources. In the past, there were tens of thousands of employees on the books; now we plan to have far fewer registered employees, but these people will be interfaces, as well as entrepreneurs. They are here to interface with huge amounts of resources. For example, take our home appliance R&D: there are 1,150 interfaces, and they interface with the external resources. Forming a relatively close layer, they tap into the more than 50,000 R&D resources, mainly made up of partners such as Baosteel (Shanghai Baoshan Iron and Steel Group). Baosteel has created a specialized R&D team for Haier; they are not there to sell steel, but to sell services, participating in Haier's front-end design. Then the next layer outwards is a relatively loose network of 1.2 million R&D resources, and they all participate in solving problems for Haier. In this way, personnel management has changed, regardless of how many registered employees do how many tasks, the registered employees are much better able to integrate human resources, so they can create a multiplier effect, attracting more online staff.

The godfather of American entrepreneurship, Howard Stevenson, defines entrepreneurship as the ability to identify opportunities beyond the existing resources, while those opportunities which everyone can see are called ventures. Haier's ventures are the autonomous ventures, the ventures created by online-registered employees, and the self-evolution mechanisms.

Autonomous ventures are very simple. In the past, superiors told staff what to do, provided the financial and human resources they needed, and asked them to report back when finished. It did not matter whether there was an effect on the market. Now there is the opportunity to discover how to self-direct so we call this self-creation, self-initiation and self-organization.

Online-registered ventures allow entrepreneurial staff to move from within the organization to outside the organization, forming an online micro-enterprise. This does away with business boundaries. People can move from registered to online, or from social resources to registered, or to online staff. One example is Sun Shengbo at Haier Mall who was originally internal to Haier, but later left to join the community of online entrepreneurs as a micro-enterprise founder with the aid of the Haier platform. He was given control of decision-making, human resources, and distribution. The final result is that the annual operating income his micro-enterprise produces is 3.5 times higher than before, and the profit growth is also very good, allowing great profit sharing.

Self-evolution mechanisms include officer self-evaluation, to bring about the best user experience, and business model evolution so that the spirit of the times can be continually captured. An example here is the direct salespeople employed by Haier in the shops. In the past, there were many direct salespeople, but now the business model has changed. We are building integrated networks focused on user interaction, so what would be the point of having so many salespeople?

Then there is the manufacturing department. In the past, the manufacturing department ran assemblies, but now it is moving away from manpower, and will move towards intelligent unmanned systems. I once visited BMW and I found that they have very few people inside their factories. We have not yet reached the level of having fully automated factories, but we are building a new manufacturing facility at Shenyang Industrial Park, at which the number of employees is already one third of the original number, and may continue to decline.

There are many such examples. I'm not talking about the concept of downsizing, because some employees were turned into micro-enterprise members, and some may have moved online. I may not employ so many R&D personnel, but online we have more R&D resources than ever before.

Two platforms

Haier's open platform restructuring has two directions of deployment, with the two listed companies in Shanghai and Hong Kong as the backbone. One is Qingdao Haier (stock code 600690), with the goal of becoming a global leader and rule maker in home appliances. Haier's five global R&D centres are resource interfaces, conducting strategic partnerships with world-class suppliers, research institutes and famous universities, forming an innovation ecosystem network of over 1.2 million scientists and engineers. By the end of 2013, Haier held more than 15,737 patent applications, with 10,167 authorized patents.

The other is the commercial network based around Haier Electronics (stock code 01169) using interactive platforms and distribution platforms, creating competitiveness via the marketing network, virtual network, logistics network and service network, providing 24-hour service, delivery and installation for customers, providing the best experience by means of virtual integration. The competitive advantage created by the convergence of these four networks will attract well-known domestic and foreign appliance brands for the distribution channel Goodaymart; the open logistics platform services the five largest e-retailers in China as well as the largest home furniture companies.

Within Haier, these are called, respectively, the 690 and 1169 Internet platforms. But Haier's platform strategy is not just a simple networked organization; platform features are also required for their products and services. On 16 January 2014, Zhang Ruimin addressed the Haier Group Interactive Internet Innovation Forum, putting forward two topics for Haier: products without the best user experience should not be produced and transactions with no value should not take place on interactive platforms.

'Products without the best user experience should not be produced' is targeted at the 690 platform and requires that appliances are transformed into smart home solutions, turning hardware into software, so that every piece of hardware has a chip, and each chip is an interactive terminal, turning household appliances into an interactive network of devices. Haier is building the Haier intelligent life platform, and the direction of the evolution is from appliances to network control, human-computer interaction, machine environment interaction, and custom self-learning.

Liang Haishan, 690 Platform Leader, appreciates that no business can completely rely on any product, or generation of products to succeed, especially for home appliances, where the products upgrade very fast, and where it is more important that the innovative system is open, and the top priority is to create a platform to interact with the user. On this platform, users constantly complain and talk about their experience of the product, so companies can understand the needs of users, allowing iterative development. Development is not just based around a particular product, but the aim will always be to attract a large number of users. So, Liang Haishan pointed out that products with no interaction are not products for the Internet age; all products must become cloud terminals.

In Haier's manufacturing great emphasis is put on 'iterations', trying to change the original 'product first, sales later' models by interacting constantly with users, and improving the products. In the past, Haier learned from Japan, but now the Japanese R&D situation is that all products must be flawlessly perfect before reaching the market, so the lead time is very long. Now Haier must immediately launch products based on user requirements, and then modify them according to their feedback. There is a saying in Silicon Valley: 'If you put the first generation product onto the market and do not feel ashamed, then you launched it too late.' Designers no longer think about things behind closed doors, but instead act on user needs.

'Transactions with no value should not take place on interactive platforms' was targeted at the 1169 platform. This was designed as 'an interactive value platform based on the virtual and simulated world', consisting of three components: first, the interactive stage, where users are involved in product design, and customer value is created; second, the transaction stage, connecting the Internet, apps, and mobile phone terminals, as well as offline physical resources, so that users can find experience centres anytime, anywhere; and third, the distribution stage, with the integration of delivery and installation, and the provision of many value-added services. In the words of Zhou Yunjie, Head of 1169, 'the dumb parts of the Internet economy have been transformed, creating value from the user interaction while simultaneously providing services to the users'.

Haier has an interactive online platform and more than 30,000 offline stores, so they can achieve an excellent user interaction experience. Looking at it a different way, users can also participate in the entire program of customization, and can customize their products and solutions. In this way, a value creating interactive platform has been developed for the interaction and transaction stages. This platform not only provides Haier services, but can also provide services for the whole of society; there are foreign home appliance brands now operating on the platform, as well as many furniture, building and decoration brands.

In fact, the open platform business is just a part of Haier's platform architecture. The ultimate goal of the networked organization is to create a passage between user resources and personalized production, making the vision of the 'big organization, micro-enterprise' real.

Zhang Ruimin – No interaction, no Haier

What is the best user experience for a product? For our free-standing air conditioners user interaction was carried out during the design stage, and this continued until the end of the process. Interaction with the users happened throughout the entire process. There are still some companies producing products for which interaction does not take place, or where the design is done behind closed doors, and after the design, advertising is produced. Today, traditional advertising should not be used at all; there shouldn't be any. If you advertise, that means there is a distance between you and the users, and you believe that the advertisement can attract users. This is simply not good enough – you must interact with users through the Internet.

Buying and selling transactions are meaningless, and run counter to the trends. They simply should not exist. Currently, Chinese e-commerce only involves transactions on price, and there is no experience of interaction. In the experience economy era, users are participants in the whole process. Americans call this the experience economy, I think the term makes sense, as the user is no longer a buyer, but has become a participant. Enterprises need to provide the best experience for the user during the entire process.

The Internet era has come; technology should not just be compared with other technology, but should be assessed to see what kind of user experience can be created. For example, looking at the rapid rise of Xiaomi, how much innovative technical content is there in Xiaomi phones? If they were competing on cell phone hardware alone, who could they beat? We should ask, when can Haier bring the best user experience in the world to customers? That is the most important thing.

The fundamental purpose of business is not to make money. So what is the fundamental purpose of business? It is to create users. Imagine a two-dimensional graph with a vertical and horizontal axis. The horizontal axis is substantially the same as other general businesses, we call this 'enterprise value', the market goals, in short, to create customers. Customers and users are not the same thing, and should be separated –'customers' make a onetime transaction with the enterprise: you make a product, the customer buys it, you hand it over, and there is no further contact; 'users', on the other hand, interact with you, are brand loyal and give their opinions, so you can continue to improve. So, the horizontal axis is customers, and the vertical axis is users, we call this the 'value network'. The vertical axis fully shows how you are creating users. In the Internet era, this is interaction with users.

We changed the perspective. In the past I would ask about our market share. I would ask how many tens of thousands of products we had sold, and whether the market share had reached 20 per cent, but things are different now, we are now concerned about whether those 20 per cent of users are interacting with us. If there are none, the user is only a customer and not a user. We used to say that making money was the end of the sales process, but now that is the start of a new sales process. In the past, users were just purchasers, whereas now users have become participants.

In the past there may not have been any interaction, but there was a kind of gaming. This so-called gaming could apply to suppliers, for example, around the price, meaning we would use whoever was cheapest; the relationship with the user is more like a marketing game, where the question is how we can use promotional materials to make you believe in our products. Because of information asymmetry, whoever communicates most is more likely to get the user's favour; for the employees, the game may be about getting more control, how to strengthen the enterprise development by controlling employees. So, we first need to change our concepts, changing from gaming to interaction, and we want interaction in every aspect, so all the interactions add value.

Thirty years of Haier

Creating the Tianzun air conditioner through interaction

Facilitating interaction is a compulsory exercise for the current transition period. For an Internet business interaction may be a natural ability, but for manufacturing enterprises accustomed to single value chains from the production line to the user, interaction is something, which must be learned.

On 3 November 2012, CCTV News Network reported on Haier's Tianzun air conditioner because it had been created as a result of interaction between Haier's employees and users. The Tianzun 'wind-tunnel' was a revolutionary air conditioning design concept that eradicated the risk of Legionnaire's disease being spread by the new unit.

Lei Yongfeng's team

Tianzun LGT head Lei Yongfeng recalls the interaction process behind the product, during which his most memorable experience was gradually working out how to interact with users. The team began their research on big data platforms such as Baidu, and found that users' number one concern about air conditioning was the risk of Legionnaire's disease. Their goal became to produce an air conditioning unit with no risk of disease.

Haier hit a wall though because users were not interacting. Either they did not come onto the available platform, or did not communicate while on the platform; Lei Yongfeng tried awarding prizes, tried using an interactive ambassador and other mechanisms, but nothing seemed to capture the attention of users as required. Eventually, Lei Yongfeng's team started looking for opinion leaders on blogs. After having interactive experiences, 'Spy' and other creative interaction tools were released, until eventually a total of nearly 700,000 users were involved. User resources provided great inspiration for the team and as Lei Yongfeng said at the time, 'If we come up with the first solution for Legionnaire's disease, then we could be the industry leader.'

The other noteworthy aspect of the Tianzun air conditioner design process was resources being used in parallel. Marketing nodes were already participating during the development phase through the interaction with users, and the manufacturing nodes were also involved as the design of the unit was begun at the same time.

Other parallel resources were the first-level resources, in which many world-class resources were directly involved in user interaction. The goal was to provide users with an air conditioning solution that could solve the problem of Legionnaires' disease. So, among those first-class resources participating in the interactions some resources, such as the Power College, had absolutely no air conditioning experience at all.

In order to continue to attract first-class resources, Lei Yong-feng's team needed the resources to be divided into five categories. For example, design resources care about the fact that only a large company like Haier will be able to apply for international design awards such as the Red Dot Design Award. The Tianzun attracted a total of 33 first-class resources.

The new air conditioner relied on the use of air jet technology. Haier's original R&D department was not equipped to work with this technology but despite this the prototype was produced within one year – twice as fast as previous developments.

Of great help in this was the fact that Haier had created a global R&D resource integration platform. This platform integrates the world's 100,000 best known universities, experts, and research institutions, involving electronics, biotechnology, power and information, so all Haier needed to do was put their R&D demands onto the platform and then wait for the research resources to come to their door.

According to Program Director of Haier Future Innovation Centre Zhang Lichen, and Vertical Air Conditioner Planning Director Lei Yongfeng: 'Around a week after the air conditioning problem was put onto the resource platform, some of the world's leading resources provided appropriate solutions. The outlet was designed by the Chinese Academy of Sciences and China Aerodynamics Research and Development and contained an intelligent module which was designed by some of the American resources.'

Using the patent or commissioning development model, Haier formed a community of interests with the world's top R&D teams. During the development process a patent pool was formed in which patents could be put into the pool, and the risks and rewards were shared depending on the proportions of the different patents used in the final product.

In the traditional manufacturing process, R&D, design, and manufacture are performed in a linear fashion. Haier proposed changing this into a parallel, fully open platform, so that all participants were involved in all aspects, and could participate simultaneously. This meant that there were no problems with nodes connecting with each other, instead they all worked at the same time in an integrative relationship. The result of this project was the Tianzun, a forward-looking, smart phone controlled air conditioner, featuring a wind-tunnel design. In terms of the marketing model, the Tianzun had been pre-ordered in advance via the Internet, and although the air conditioner cost up to ¥20,000, on 31 December 2013, 1,228 units were sold through the e-commerce platform alone.

The head of the 65-strong team temporarily working on the Tianzun said that the emergence of the unit could be thought of as a great example of the broader transformation of Haier. From the difficult and arduous interactions, starting with no prior expectations, to allowing the user needs to enter the product design, the entire process revealed a manufacturer who was determined to employ a network model based around the Internet.

Everyone is a maker

Zhang Ruimin was deeply influenced by Chris Anderson. During the first half of 2014, when Anderson visited Haier, Zhang Ruimin broke down Anderson's work, talking about the core of each book as well as his own personal experience.

He felt that Anderson's *Makers* read like a prophecy for the future – a maker can subvert a company. However, it would be extremely difficult to achieve this vision. Zhang Ruimin asked Anderson whether, if you created an enterprise of makers, after its initial success, the company could still operate like a maker company. Anderson said it would not be possible, as it would return to being a traditional company, from architecture to the supply chain.

Zhang Ruimin means the term 'maker' to have an entrepreneurial connotation, it is not just intended to suggest people involved in manufacturing. A key concept for the organization of the Haier platform is the idea that everyone is a maker. In other words, allowing Haier employees to go into business on the Haier platform, and allowing them to learn all about Haier.

When several business people get together, that becomes a micro-enterprise. The term began to be used by Haier in the second half of 2013, as a new organizational concept. It is a means to allow all Haier employees to become makers. Within Haier, the term does not refer to the micro-business you might find in general business terminology, limited by the number of people and operational turnover, but refers to businesses created and grown on Haier's business program, by a group of makers, which could be two or three people, but could be 20 or 30 people, or even 200 or 300 people. Only three or four people are involved in the micro-enterprise Thunderobot, while the Smart Shenyang Plant micro-enterprise involves hundreds of people.

The micro-enterprise concept is likely to gradually replace ZZJYTs. Some micro-enterprises are indeed players who have grown up in the new market – for example, Thunderobot laptops, Air Boxes and Water Boxes. Some micro-enterprises such as Shenyang factory are 'micro' in the spiritual meaning of the word only: it tells employees that their every initiative and innovation could be disruptive.

Of course, the goal of the platformization of Haier is to subvert the entire manufacturing process, and micro-enterprises are just the first step. Allowing employees to have an entrepreneurial spirit is the only way to develop makers who can really show disruptive capability in the future.

Zhang Ruimin thinks that the changes at the company are only deepening. In 2013, while stressing the individual goals together business model, Zhang Ruimin announced his vision for Haier employees: 'Everyone is a CEO.' Individual goals together require very smooth processes and the flow of these processes will inevitably lead to the increased complexity of the value-added work. One person facing the market is like a traditional business process facing the market, even if the non-value added work was reduced, some basic bonding work still needs to be done. Employees are not only required to have a strong driving force, but also need to develop the ability of a CEO to offer complex services. Those accustomed to the way of thinking common in large companies – with staff not thinking outside of their own position – must now face the market with a strong business philosophy, taking the perspective of the company in interacting with customers.

In 2014, after clarifying the direction of Haier as a platform-based organization, Zhang Ruimin proposed the slogan 'everyone is a maker'. In fact, the final status after the enterprise-wide reconstruction will likely be a system in which individuals can directly use the power of the company to achieve their own personal goals. Achieving this will push the traditional company to go beyond 'organizational containers', as the enterprise will have turned into a social platform. This enables Haier's subversion formula, in which everyone moves from creating products to creating makers.

Who are the makers? This is the key question. Zhang Ruimin stresses the two-way aspect of this concept, that is, tradition can only create innovators within the organization, but now, online entrepreneurs are also available; at the same time, social resources can come into Haier, starting online and registered businesses. If 'everyone is a CEO', then from an enterprise perspective, 'everyone is a maker' is the obvious result. It is clear that Zhang Ruimin has intentionally erased organizational boundaries, emphasizing the trend of the organization towards society.

'Individual goals together', 'ZZJYTs' and 'makers' are all pointing to one goal – self-motivation and self-management. In time, Haier hopes to turn itself into a large community.

Zhang Ruimin, at the 2014 innovation annual meeting raising the idea that 'Everyone is a Maker'

Thirty years of Haier

Liang Haishan – from execution to innovation

When he joined Haier in 1988, Liang Haishan may have been the only company member who had encountered 'management' at university. Liang Haishan graduated from Xi'an Jiaotong University with a major in Management Engineering. This major was separate from those issued by the Department of Mechanical Engineering, as the Department of Mechanical Machinery was based around professional manufacturing. After identifying the fact that a machinery plant must have management, industrial design, logistics and other aspects of design, the Management Engineering major was separated from the other courses. Xi'an Jiaotong University and Tsinghua University were the first in China to create Schools of Management, so we could say that China's enterprise management started from factory management. Students were told that

they would be trained to be factory heads, but after gradua-
tion, only Liang Haishan entered a factory.

Shortly after his workshop practice period was concluded,
he was assigned to the Office of Management, responsible
for corporate and regulatory reform. At that time, Haier was
engaged in two-way selection and competition for employment, proposing performance-related pay; this was very
advanced for the time in China. He then moved to the team
that was involved in preparations to list the company.

Liang Haishan was responsible for combing through the internal mechanisms and the adoption of information technology,
so he may have been the first person to need to understand
Zhang Ruimin's reforms:

> Haier has always been on the path of change and
> transformation, but today's strategy of enterprise plat-
> formization, employee – makers and user individualization
> requires us to upgrade our transformation method. But for
> me the question was how to go from the original following
> of innovation to the implementation of innovation, then to
> transition to today's self-innovation – this was the biggest
> challenge.

After, the thirtieth anniversary of the Group, Liang Haishan, the
rotating president, said of his role in the transitions: 'Whether
they are external or internal, resources can interact in the innovation ecosystem, so all employees can become makers, they
can even generate business with users.' Liang Haishan admits
that this change is much larger than any in the past, with a
deeper magnitude, and wider range, placing more responsibility than ever before on individuals. If Haier people only knew
how to implement the Group strategy, it would no longer meet
the requirements of the Group, so everyone must become an
independent innovator instead of a strategic executor – copy-
ing must become creation.

Transformation cannot be a kind of static transformation; one cannot stop and wait for a successful transition, but must grow and transform at the same time, so as to achieve enterprise development as well as personal development. Liang Haishan said that this has created a lot of pressure. Business operators have to deal with two forces on a day-to-day basis: the stretching force generated by users and the thrust from the organization. The higher the compatibility of these two kinds of force, the better the enterprise can develop. So how should an enterprise deal with these two forces? The answer is to promote the organization to become a platform for innovation, such that this innovation platform allows unlimited interaction with the user. Saying yes to user requirements, and not worrying about our own needs is always the way to solve this problem. In fact, companies should only have one track, the user track. Making the adjustments to get onto this track, then being able to precisely follow along the track means that the enterprise has sustainable genes. Trends in future user requirements determined the arrival of the user solution era.

Looking back over the past 30 years, Liang Haishan's greatest satisfaction was the feeling of closely following the changes in user behaviour:

Haier has been working on the high-speed subversion of normal practices, from the late 1980s when we introduced two-way competitive selection for job positions, to the market process re-engineering, and then to the zero inventory concept in 2008. These were all transformations to allow the company to better respond to the needs of the user.

Each step of Haier's subsequent development proves this desire to subvert norms – the transformation at each stage accurately responded to changes in user needs. I sometimes think that if I had thoroughly understood this somewhat earlier, the results of the implementation would have been better, and the organizational costs to the enterprise would have been lower.

The most impressive thing was the 2008 zero inventory revolution.

Liang Haishan recalls that in August of that year, the Group decided to use the 'zero inventory, instant supply as demand rises' model. At that time, the next sales quarter was quickly approaching, and the company had to ensure that the results were not affected, while also achieving 'zero inventory' at the same time. These two opposing forces were extremely demanding. 'Since the Group had a clear strategy, we had to fully implement it, and after a month of fighting, we successfully resolved the contradiction.' Later, when the global financial crisis hit, the advantages of the new Haier model could be clearly seen.

'In fact, we were the beneficiaries of these changes, because they took us to a new arena. Big changes bring big arenas, whereas small changes bring small ones.' Liang Haishan concludes that, 'enterprises have to capture the spirit of the times, and individuals have to integrate into the arena of business change. As makers, we can enjoy dancing on the broader platform offered by Haier, so we can really find our own roles.'

As the head of a large platform, people must become a maker and the protector of an ecosystem. Liang Haishan believes that in the Internet era, the concept of 'leadership' is already falling behind the times. The only person who can dictate to employees is the user, and the only environment capable of bringing about the value of the employee is an excellent business ecosystem; therefore, employees have been allowed to become units of change, and numerous micro-enterprises have emerged. The heads of large platforms must construct an ecosystem for the continued emergence and rapid development of micro-enterprises, allowing them to evolve, self-optimize and self-manage, so that each one follows its own user track.

Zhang Ruimin – Haier only has three types of people

There are only three types of people at Haier: heads of platforms, heads of micro-enterprises, and members of micro-enterprises.

The platform heads build a platform, and do two things:

1. Transition to the new Internet model after the original structure and workflow are eliminated, otherwise there will be no new order in place when the original order is broken, which would result in chaos.

2. Make sure that the platform is open. When new people can freely join, we say 'first grade resources can freely enter' and 'maximized benefits to all parties', because if each party gets the maximum benefit, we are more likely to attract people to join. Once something is open, people will not allow it to be closed again.

The head of a micro-enterprise is the head of an entrepreneurial team. This team enjoys the decisions-making right, the right to employ staff and distribution rights, and can use social resources and capital for their entrepreneurship.

The others are members of the micro-enterprises. They are not the fixed workers of the past, but are undergoing the process of becoming 'online' staff (as opposed to registered staff). Now, staff churn is relatively high. We have a saying that 'officers and soldiers are mutually selected': if the officers feel the soldiers are not acceptable, they can find other people to join the team; if the soldiers feel the officers are not acceptable, they can remove the officers.

Within the company we now have 200 micro-enterprises. However, only about 10 per cent of those are really 'socialized'.

To truly become makers is not an easy thing, not only do

underlying concepts need to be changed, but we also need to provide them with various resources, especially benefits. Originally, we had many mid-level staff, but now we have none of those positions, and the wage system has changed. In September 2005, we started the individual goals together concept. The process was implemented over a very long time because it was really very difficult. After all, there were tens of thousands of people in the company to pay and the whole payment system was being overhauled.

Now some people are completely paid for their maker activity. The so-called 'maker payment' works like this: a maker sets goals; generally speaking it's a three-year development goal, which is split to annual and monthly targets. According to those targets, that maker can get the appropriate remuneration. One way is called 'profit sharing', in which the maker creates above-the-target profits, which can be shared; another way is to grant certain shares and get returns on investment: this is what we call 'socialized'.

Micro-enterprise makers

Zhang Ruimin has said, 'eggs broken from the outside will be someone's dinner, but an egg broken from the inside will bring new life to the world'. Turning the fixed staff into makers is really a way of allowing the system to be broken from the inside, turning the organization of the large enterprise into a closely linked collection of micro-enterprises, which constitute an ecosystem for Haier.

Haier was China's earliest manufacturing company to raise the idea of moving from being factory-centric, with a large-scale B2C production model, into becoming a consumer-centric, flexible production and precise C2B service model. The individual goals together win-win model is the foundation of the micro-enterprises, that is, employees have the right to make their own policies based on market changes, and employees have the right to determine their own income based on the user value they manufacture.

Zhang Ruimin raised the Network Strategy as the guideline for the fifth stage of Haier's strategic development, thereby turning Haier into a platform-based organization and achieving the goals of 'business with no borders', 'management with no leadership' and 'scale-free supply chain'. Business without borders emphasizes the fact that the organization is no longer closed; management without leadership means that the staff must be self-driven and self-managed, in fact it can be understood as the predecessor to the idea of makers; supply chain without scales refers to the interfaces with external resources. The three combined make the micro-enterprises.

Zhang Ruimin believes that any of the two basic business operations (value creation and transfer of value), or the three flows (information flow, capital flow and logistics) require their own entrepreneurship and innovation. What does not exist any more is an exclusively executive node.

Haier tries to include all employees in one of four types of micro-enterprise: virtual, incubation, transformation or ecological.

The focus of the virtual micro-enterprises is to change thinking; what they are engaged in is still the original business, but the ways of thinking and working should be adapted to the new era. The incubation micro-enterprises are focused on creating new projects; the business they are engaged in did not originally exist elsewhere. Transformation micro-enterprises are focused on new models; these micro-enterprises have grown to some extent, and have their own products and markets, but as the external market changes, they need to change and operate with a new model. Ecosystem micro-enterprises are maker projects added to the Haier platform and ecosystem that have no direct relationship with the enterprise in the traditional way, but they work, create value and innovate within the Haier ecosystem.

The four types of micro-enterprise include all staff, so for Haier employees, they either join a micro-enterprise, or they are dismissed.

This was a trial and error process, and the transition was not allowed to produce a decline in performance. During this micro-enterprise process, Haier had the following three issues, which urgently needed to be addressed:

1. The products of the micro-enterprises were focused around breakthroughs in technology, but there was still a lack of 'phenomenal' products. Redefinitions of products are a difficult problem for the entire appliance industry.

2. The main incentives for the platform head (whose responsibility is to bring about more micro-enterprises) supporting micro-enterprises are not clear. Those middle managers in the traditional organizational structure would feel the greatest impact from the changes. On the one hand their role was changing dramatically, while on the other hand, the question of how to adapt to those changes and complete the transition was not yet clear.

3. Although Haier's platform is still under construction, the ecological structure is approaching completion and there is now a lack of high-quality resources. In other words, the question is how to attract people. Since the company was not very open in the past, and since there was a lack of Internet experience, Haier needed to gain experience in resource development and identification. High-quality resources are an important part of the Haier platform strategy.

The key now is that Haier needs to hatch a number of really small micros. The principle is that they operate independently, and share risk and profit, driven by the external market and users, and reflecting this by improving product innovation and performance.

Thirty years of Haier

Water boxes and the clean water platform

The Water Box is an app based water purifier companion device that allows users to conduct real-time water quality checks and reminds them to replace water purification filters, while also offering a range of other useful features. Its biggest feature is that it is completely original, as there are currently no similar products at home or abroad.

The idea for the Water Box was generated from interaction with users. Previously, the Haier Water Equipment Department carried out the manufacturing and sales business. They launched an online platform to communicate with users, which was divided into several chat topics. Inspiration for the Water Box came from the chat topic about water quality monitoring.

In recent years, Chinese people have become more concerned about water and air quality and safety. However, this did not fit with the actual conditions one found for China. The current installation rate in the foreign developed market for water purification systems was up to 92 per cent, while China's water purification installation rate was less than 2 per cent. This data reflects the huge potential of the Chinese water market, while also reflecting confusion over the current development of that market. Although increasing numbers of users have begun installing home water purification equipment, the equipment's effect on water cannot be perceived by users, so how can it be measured? When should the filter in a water purifier be replaced? Users had no answers to these problems, which were the very problems they were most concerned about.

These points became popular topics of discussion among the water quality monitoring chat groups. At that time, the Haier water purifier Director of Planning Zou Hao, was responsible for this group. He began to look into finding a way to resolve the user problems. This coincided with the 'maker' reform at the

Haier Group within which Haier provided platform resources for micro-entrepreneurs, to enable everyone to become a maker.

The deep understanding of user needs and the company incentive mechanisms combined to enable Zou Hao to become an entrepreneur. This choice meant that Zou Hao had to give up his salary, and take only a small basic wage. But at the same time, if the project developed well, Zou Hao would be able to obtain more of the value of his idea. Facing this risk, Zou Hao chose to gamble on his idea, and signed a schedule agreement. He became the head of a micro-enterprise.

Zou Hao persuaded another colleague to join him. From program design, mould design, resource sourcing and production, Zou Hao and colleagues advanced rapidly, using the speed of the Internet. Although they were still within Haier Park, they had been transformed into entrepreneurs. Zou Hao said that this was totally different to working at the company as he had in the past, 'The Water Box had a module which needed to be integrated. Conventional thinking would mean waiting for the company to advance.' But after founding our own business, the team immediately used its own personal connections to find the resources.

The entrepreneurship mentality of doing overtime took over, yet still Zou Hao took three months to come up with his solution: a smart box which can test water quality. It took three months to achieve the transformation from innovation to product; this would have been unthinkable using the traditional manufacturing model. Zou Hao, using internal entrepreneurial mechanisms and the Internet, emerged out of the era of traditional thinking, and created the product in a very short period of time.

In addition to manufacturing, Zou Hao and his colleagues adapted the Internet method and brought it into their pricing and marketing processes. Following the traditional pricing system, after accounting, the price of the Water Box would be around ¥499. In the Internet era, you need to consider what the acceptable range for product pricing is for the users. Feedback can be obtained via online research, and the Water Box was pre-sold online, where it was found that the users would generally accept a price point of ¥299.

To date, 80,000 units of the original Water Box have been sold. The second generation Water Box, and a range of other products, are in the planning or manufacturing stage.

Zou Hao's Water Box project required setting up the company Hao Hai Science and Technology. In addition to the investment of the Haier Group, he also personally invested ¥400,000. At the same time, the company also attracted additional capital and resources. Zou Hao said the current distribution mechanism for the project is very clear, the Haier Group signed a schedule of targets or sales goals with them, and after the completion of the targets, any extra value would be shared by the company. Regarding future developments, Zou Hao talks about his hope that in three years time they will achieve a scale that will make it desirable for the Haier Group to repurchase them. Water Box, from being an internal venture, has become a real micro-enterprise.

The Water Box micro-business evolved from the water purifier micro-business. The water purifier LGT interface Qu Jianan was Zou Hao's line leader. Now, Qu Guinan has became a shareholder in Zou Hao's business on behalf of the water purifier platform. Just as Zou Hao became the head of the micro-enterprise, so Qu Guinan was transformed into a micro-enterprise partner.

And Qu Guinan is also entrepreneurial – he had previously observed that Haier water purification products were aimed at industry, and that they did not understand the needs of domestic users. In August 2012, Qu Guinan competed to become one of the heads of a Haier LGT project, and his inter-active water platform formally launched on 23 September, by running Test the Water Quality activities. He hoped to create a data set about local water quality based on wide-scale water testing, including testing water in users' own homes. Currently, there is data for more than 220,000 districts on the platform, covering 200 million households, and this data is freely and openly available.

This has obvious sales benefits for Haier as those users who dis-cover that they have poor water quality will probably choose to buy the water purification system Haier offers for their par-ticular situation, and possibly a Water Box to go with it. In early 2013, Qu Guinan promised to reach an annual sales target of ¥150 million, but by the end of the year, he had over delivered. The platform brings about a virtuous cycle of added value. This is a very important characteristic of the platform – it must be capable of self-enhancement.

In addition to the Water Box micro-enterprise, Qu Guinan's water purifier platform is currently hatching another three micro-enterprises targeting different user groups. During the incubation process, Qu Guinan found that different micro-enterprises have different characteristics, and the market mechanisms are also different. For instance, he is currently hatching a micro-enterprise that will bring about marketization through a joint investment approach.

The process of marketizing micro-enterprises will continue to face new challenges, but Qu Guinan says even so, he must allow the independence of the micro-enterprises. Qu Guinan has also discovered that no decisions should be made behind closed doors. Everything has to be open, incorporating both user interaction and the adoption of Internet thinking, allowing the participation of external professional resources.

Zou Hao and Qu Guinan's business story is an interesting example of the micro-enterprise incubation platform. The

Haier interactive water platform is connected in parallel. Users are at the top, but suppliers are also at the top; all the necessary foreign and domestic brands are on the platform, and they all interact. Also, through interaction, the platform has become an ecosystem, allowing customers and suppliers to find points of interest, excitement and ways to benefit.

Eliminate the middle

On 14 June 2014, Zhang Ruimin delivered a speech at the Wharton Global Forum. He turned to the question of corporate middle management: 'At the beginning of last year Haier had 86,000 middle managers, but by late last year that fell to 70,000, a decrease of 18 per cent. This year we expect to remove a further 10,000, mainly from the middle layers. As our business processes become more intelligent, we will need fewer people.'

His remarks caused a huge uproar. Articles appeared in the media talking about layoffs, and Haier and Zhang Ruimin both suffered huge criticism. 'Haier is not bearing its social responsibility', 'it has gone through too radical a change' and 'Zhang Ruimin is becoming incompetent' were among the criticisms voiced. Despite the doubters, Zhang Ruimin remained firm: 'The existence of the middle layers in an organization should relate to the purpose of the organization, as well as to the organization's objectives. I want to turn the organization into an ecosystem, consisting of many small organizations, so what would be the purpose of a middle layer of management?'

When Zhang Ruimin began to promote the idea that everyone is a maker, the first challenge was the question of how to resolve the remuneration issue. Haier had been using a broadband pay structure and changing this was a very difficult thing to do. Formerly, middle managers had fixed job levels and remuneration and subsidies with finite ranges, so it was all very clear. Of course, there were assessments, and pay levels were reduced if performance was poor. If the performance was good on the other hand, compensation could be increased, but there was not much movement either way. During the organizational changes at Haier, the company had only looked at who had more user resources, because the salary was changed to being based on the user resources and user value held by the middle managers, becoming both flexible and fuzzy. A consulting company put a lot of effort into helping Haier to implement a hierarchical pay system, but this had become an obstacle to change.

Zhang Ruimin ran some calculations: 'Salary reform involved many thousands of people. Within the whole Group, there were 5,681 grade seven people, 1,141 grade eight people, and 320 grade nine people, so if the pay reform was not handled correctly, it would cause many problems.' However, he was determined that the broadband pay system must be completely overthrown, even if a dual-track program would have to be introduced.

Building on the experience with the ZZJYTs, Zhang Ruimin wanted to take the original intermediate levels, that is, second-level ZZJYTs, and gradually integrate these into grade one ZZJYTs, bringing about compensation uniformity. If grade one staff earn no money, then there is no source of money for grade two staff. The original single pay system has now gradually changed so that everyone is profit sharing, that is, if there are no extra profits there is nothing to share, but you are allowed to try to attract resources from the community. For example, some micro-enterprises have looked to the community to provide financial assistance, probably making a few hundred yuan a month, so they did not have to access the company's finances.

Not surprisingly, during the time when the ZZJYTs were being trialled relatively large resistance was encountered from level two staff. Many middle managers said they had reformed into an inverted triangle structure, but in fact a lot of things had changed in name only. Zhang Ruimin was troubled by this, and concerned that if Haier continued to allow the existence of grade two staff, his organizational transformation could not be completed.

In fact, there exists an inherent paradox: Zhang Ruimin's

decision was to turn the enterprise structure from a triangle into an inverted triangle; but more force was required to implement this change. Zhang Ruimin would normally have relied on the middle level of management, but these people were themselves the targets of the revolution.

Zhang Ruimin believes that this is an example of Max Weber's bureaucracy. At first bureaucracy is the force of national stability, but it then becomes the nation's resistance to change. If countries wish to be stable, they rely on it, but if they want to change, they cannot get rid of it. Zhang Ruimin believed that this dilemma of bureaucracy had not been solved in the past. But, in the Internet era, he hoped he could find a new solution: the question facing Zhang Ruimin was how the network organization could subvert Weber's centralized administrative bureaucracy. At its core, the enterprise is a user-driven business.

Haier used two properties of the Internet – networking and platforming – to subvert the division of labour as well as hierarchy. Looking at networking, Zhang Ruimin says its biggest difference from hierarchies is the zero distance aspect. In *Management Challenges of the Twenty-first Century* Peter Drucker noted that the biggest contribution of the Internet is the elimination of distance. This meant that lines and bureaucracy must be changed. The platform is a way to quickly configure resources, so that they can be deployed through the platform. This represents the destruction and subversion of bureaucracy, because bureaucratic organizations restrict the rapid allocation of resources.

In the final analysis, what Haier achieved was not an elimination of the middle, but a complete flattening of the organization. After flattening, Haier had fewer leaders, and everyone was joined on a platform. In the conversion process, Zhang Ruimin raised the 'organizational theory of threes':

1. Marketization of relationships. The relationships between departments, upward and downward relationships as well as peer relationships, have all become market relationships.

2. Information monetization. Organizations need someone who

is responsible for making information generate value.

3. Resource liberalization. This must be established on the basis of the two previous items, as it is the highest level of platform organization.

In order to bring about resource liberalization, Zhang Ruimin adjusted the individual remuneration previously used at Haier, the individual order and payment table and introduced 'remuneration for orders'. It changes the sequence of 'people – order – payment' to 'order – people – payment'. The market is in front, and people are behind that. Zhang Ruimin says: 'In the past we had to first consider the individuals and how to call on their ability to take on the orders. That is not necessary now, because if you cannot do it, we will find new people.'

Rebirth after suicide or death

Thunderobot is one of Haier's gaming notebook computers, and was one of the many items created on the Haier platform. Zhao Yanbing and Li Ning were key to its development.

In order to be able to develop a product which could truly meet customer needs, Zhao Yanbing and Li Ning collected more than 300,000 BBS (bulletin board system) reviews of gaming notebooks from the websites of e-commerce providers and performed an organized analysis of the comments. From this process they were able to identify the 13 most common problems, including overheating, proneness to crashing and frequent blue screens. They felt that they had the ability to meet seven of these issues, or user requirements.

So, in the absence of any formal sales, the Thunderobot team first started advertising in JD Mall, saying that interested people could join a WeChat group. Those who came forward became the original Thunderobot fans. Two continuous generations of products were equipped with a VIP card. This card was a pass allowing entry to the WeChat group to become a fan. The Thunderobot official WeChat group totalled 500 people, and five groups were spontaneously formed under the group, making a total of more than 2,000 die-hard fans.

Li Ning, who was responsible for interaction with fans, concluded that Thunderobot fans could be divided into the following categories: guides, who are very sincere and will give suggestions on the marketing strategy; talkers, those with emotional needs, who chat about a variety of topics, even intimate topics, and who will give very detailed responses to questions; and fevered fans, who are very enthusiastic about gaming equipment, and will carefully explain the major problems. A third of the fan base were born after 1990, and most grew up in homes with no shortage of money, but with alternative lifestyles.

These fans frequently interacted with Li Ning well into the night. The number of fans was close to the maximum that Li Ning could handle alone, they needed to be self-managing. The Thunderobot team designed and provided a range of mechanisms, rewarding the contributions of 'fan leaders', but also encouraging other fans to contribute to the community. Thunderobot gives fans a title, so that they automatically form a kind of pecking order, such as the Baidu Teiba Forum Owner, the Captain of a Group and so on.

The way for fans to be recognized is much more attractive than material rewards. Fans actively participate in community activities, and create their own accessories, uploading wallpapers they have produced, along with installation tutorials, evaluations, related news and so on, just to get the recognition and respect of other fans.

The fans have formed a self-governing Thunderobot fan community with a strong capacity to evolve and solid group cohesion. The Thunderobot's fast-growing community of fans now numbers almost 1 million.

The loyalty of the fans is a recognition of something that would not have happened without a series of interactions. Haier feels they are a famous brand, but as Li Ning communicated with users he found that the children of the 1990s do not recognize brands, but only recognize performance. Removing the Haier brand reduced the distance from users.

When it came to production, gamers unanimously approved of the production quality of the Lantian plant. Haier had cooperated a few years before with this plant on an overseas project, but the results were not ideal. The scope of Lantian was slightly too small when compared to Haier, and they did not even meet the required standards in some aspects. At the same time, the OEM price was high, but Lantian would not break with its rules for such a small customer as Thunderobot. Li Ning continued to send the user comments to Lantian, and even invited the Lantian designers to enter the group and participate in some chats. This, for Lantian who had stubbornly followed OEM pricing, was very moving, so they agreed. To date, the cost to performance ratio of the Thunderobot produced by Lantian, could be said to be the industry's best. And this was something that would have been simply impossible to achieve from just a brand perspective.

During the interaction, the team discovered that the fan's expectations of the graphics cards exceeded the original specifications. As a result, there was an emergency consultation with the supplier, and in a very short space of time, the configuration was upgraded.

In January 2014, when the second generation Thunderobot was released, JD Mall subscribers reached 18 million. With the conversion rate of JD Mall the Thunderobot team expected that 3,000 units would be sold, so 3,000 units were released, and money was paid in advance. In the event, the planned sales of 3,000 units were reached in just 21 minutes.

Haier, with the benefit of their own platform, looked for venture capital for the Thunderobot team, and hoped to use the introduction of venture capital to Thunderobot to bring a fresh perspective and more power. Thunderobot is a typical example of Haier's policy that 'everyone is a maker'.

Zhang Ruimin expects Haier to become a huge platform organization. He believes that the traditional organizational structure of the enterprise will completely disappear, so that anyone who wants to create customers can make use of the Haier brand, and grow on this huge platform. The goal of the makers is totally socialized, that is, the Haier brand itself does not restrict the makers in any way. For example, Thunderobot has not used the Haier brand, but has produced a new brand based on user preferences.

Zhang Ruimin also refers to his subversion as a suicide. Haier's suicide was 'de-Haierization', that is, completely saying goodbye to their previous success. Only very few companies can commit suicide, but those who can really do it, can live on forever.

Thirty years of Haier

Lu Kailin – The big gaming dream

'Without a steady stream of fans, everything is nebulous,' said Lu Kailin, head of the micro-enterprise that innovated the Haier 690 notebook. He now has a new identity, general manager of Thunderobot Technology Company in Qingdao.

When the Thunderobot gaming laptop went onto the

market, 500 units were sold within five days; for the second batch, a record of 18,000 orders, and 3,000 sales in 21 minutes was achieved. For the first pre-sales of the third incarnation, 3,000 units of the ¥6,999 Thunderobot 911 were sold within 10 seconds.

For unit sales in volume terms these numbers may not be huge, but the fact that Thunderobot gained such a strong appeal in such a short time was something the entire industry noted. Thunderobot became the star of the industry, and many people began to quietly inquire about its secrets.

Lu Kailin said: 'In fact, there are no secrets. The emergence of Thunderobot was inevitable as the notebook industry had experienced negative growth for two consecutive years. We analysed user complaints and found that existing gaming notebooks could not meet the needs of gamers in many ways. So, we decided to use our Internet thinking and operational model and apply it to the gaming notebook market.'

Thunderobot's name was also devised in collaboration with users.

When the first 500 Thunderobot products were put on the market, the user feedback included some from users saying that there were bright spots on the screen.

Lu Kailin says of this:

We began by telling them that the bright spots were normal, because state regulations consider three or fewer bright spots to be within the acceptable range. Later we decided this was not acceptable, because the user has the right to choose, so if the product does not meet their demands they can choose not to buy it. These users said they would prefer to spend another ¥300 to buy the product without bright spots; as a result, the Thunderobot team took on board the views of users, and replaced the screen display on subsequent versions.

Talking about these issues, Lu Kailin said: 'User requirements change very quickly, so in order to make a good product we must continue to interact with the user. Without a steady stream of fans to provide requirements for product strategy, everything is nebulous. There can be no sustained competitiveness.'

These experiences allowed Lu Kailin to recognize that to make successful products in the Internet era, enterprises must make a paradigm shift from thinking for the user to letting the user do the thinking, and they also have to transform workers into makers. Only by creating value for users can the team share the greater value. Therefore, in response to the Group's strategy to promote micro-enterprises, Lu Kailin's team set up a micro-enterprise.

'Now we no longer rely on the company payroll, but we spend what we earn.' Lu Kailin said the micro-enterprise has decision-making powers, power to use staff as they wish and distribution rights, so it can achieve self-management and self-optimization. 'We decide everything from product operations, staff joining and leaving, and salary distribution, so we do not have to wait for the approval of other layers. This really makes everyone very enthusiastic, so each person feels like they are developing themselves fully. Employees now rush to work, because if they cannot create value, they will have no place in the micro-enterprise.'

In JD Mall, Thunderobot is the second ranked product in the gaming category, top ranked for its average unit price. However, Lu Kailin's gaming dream is not just limited to the Thunderobot gaming notebook, he also has greater entrepreneurial dreams.

Lu Kailin said what Thunderobot wants to target is the gaming industry as a whole not just gaming notebooks. Turning to future planning he explained that products are the core, but service and absolute respect for the users behind the products is the essence of the company. Thunderobot's future includes three steps. The first step is the development direction of the hardware, how Thunderobot can develop from gaming notebooks to consoles and then onto mobile phones. The second step is software development, and entering into the gaming industry. The third step is cultural value, Thunderobot's goal is to become a professional gaming company with millions of fans.

Why do companies fail?

In March 2013, Zhang Ruimin met with Gary Hamel, one of the world's top management experts. They discussed Zhang Ruimin's ideas on change. Hamel was able to understand the logic of Haier, but could not understand where Haier's courage for change came from. Former IBM CEO Louis V. Gerstner Jr. once had the idea of subverting IBM's organizational structure, but because of the difficulties he encountered, he gave up. Given Haier's size and industry status, the company's capacity for change is undoubtedly world class.

Zhang Ruimin has said of the change processes that Haier has undergone:

> The hardest thing was that there were no benchmarks, no one we could imitate. The development of China and Chinese enterprises since the Chinese economic reform has been rapid, but it was catch-up growth, signposted growth. My biggest concern was whether we would be okay, and if not, what we should do about it. We needed a model that could stand the test of time. I would pencil things in, so if it was not okay we could go back to that model. But nobody has a tested model now. The biggest problem is that there are no signposts.

In one corner of Zhang Ruimin's office there is a *Fortune* magazine front cover, showing a ship being capsized, the headline reads: 'Why do companies fail?' Traditionally, business leaders have been likened to captains, holding binoculars up to look into the future, and establishing the long-term vision, while unswervingly moving forward. However, the more common situation today is that leaders lead people to sail into heavy impenetrable fog, and this fog envelopes the future. Zhang Ruimin believes that he is not a captain but a boat designer, enabling the enterprise to navigate whatever rough weather may be coming. The greatest pleasure for him is exploration.

Zhang Ruimin, the ship designer

Hu Yong: Your future strategy is well-diversified, but Kevin Kelly said that if control is lost, top down organization is required, or if we can use an analogy, for modern companies on the unstable seas of today, if the captain doesn't have enough control, the boat faces the risk of capsizing. I would like to hear you talk about the non-controlled, more decentralized relationships for the senior leaders in a modern business.

Zhang Ruimin: Haier has now become a number of boats. I think having one ship is very dangerous.

I think my role is neither helmsman nor captain, but boat designer. I want to be able to transform the ships, with full redesigns when required, according to the external situation, so maybe I would design one ship, or perhaps I would design many smaller boats.

Right now, it is like I have designed many small boats, and I am only in charge of the flagship, just the leading vessel of the flotilla. I only provide direction for one of the ships. In fact, everyone can move in their own forward direction, the directions are not all the same. Different paths are possible, but they will serve the same purpose.

Hu Yong: But now there are numerous boats, doesn't this increase the risks? Is there a high likelihood of success?

Zhang Ruimin: There is no positive response to this, really no positive response, because this is too difficult. The extent of this subversion means that we would be lucky not to encounter any major problems.

Hu Yong: Have you considered what you will do if you are unsuccessful? If you fail in your attempts?

Zhang Ruimin: I think it unlikely that we will see a complete failure. There may be relatively large twists and turns, but after all, there will be some sparks of success and if we fan the fire those will get larger.

Hu Yong: So, the ideal situation would be to spark a full-on fire. Would that be considered a success?

Zhang Ruimin: No, in fact, things are always moving, this would be finding order for a time only. In this chaotic world, being able to maximize value at any one time is enough. In the year when the Dow Jones Index celebrated its centenary, only one company that had been listed in 1896 remained to participate in the celebrations, only GE was left. How long had passed? Just one century.

Hu Yong: Looking through *The Pursuit of Excellence* written by Tom Peters, and even *Built to Last* by Jim Collins, you can see a few years later, many of these companies are finished. Digital Equipment Corporation, Motorola, and so on.

Zhang Ruimin: They were legends of their time, but they do not stand for long. That is just how people think, after all, people are people, how fast do external changes happen? Yet people still assume that the exterior is constant, and will not change.

I'm just exploring, I never think about what the final conse-
quences will be, I don't think about what we will do in the
future or how we will do it, we can answer those questions
when we come to them.

An image of a human explorer in the Haier museum in Qingdao